LEICESTER

A POTTED HISTORY

STEPHEN BUTT

AMBERLEY

First published 2026

Amberley Publishing
The Hill, Stroud
Gloucestershire, GL5 4EP

www.amberley-books.com

ISBN 978 1 3981 3028 9 (print)
ISBN 978 1 3981 3029 6 (ebook)

British Library Cataloguing in Publication Data.
A catalogue record for this book is available from the British Library.

Typeset by Simon and Sons ITES Services Pvt. Ltd., Chennai, India.
Printed in Great Britain.

Appointed GPSR EU Representative: Easy Access System Europe Oü, 16879218
Address: Mustamäe tee 50, 10621, Tallinn, Estonia
Contact Details: gpsr.requests@easproject.com, +358 40 500 3575

Contents

Introduction

History is more than a record of past events. It is a dynamic narrative shaped by interpretation, consequences and the experiences of people. History provides the backdrop against which the present unfolds, and our understanding of it is inevitably influenced by the lens of contemporary life.

In Leicester, history speaks to us not only through written records but also through the architecture, the road network and even the nuances of the local dialect. From the façade of a modern department store to the footpaths across Jubilee Square, the history is there for us to see, hear and touch.

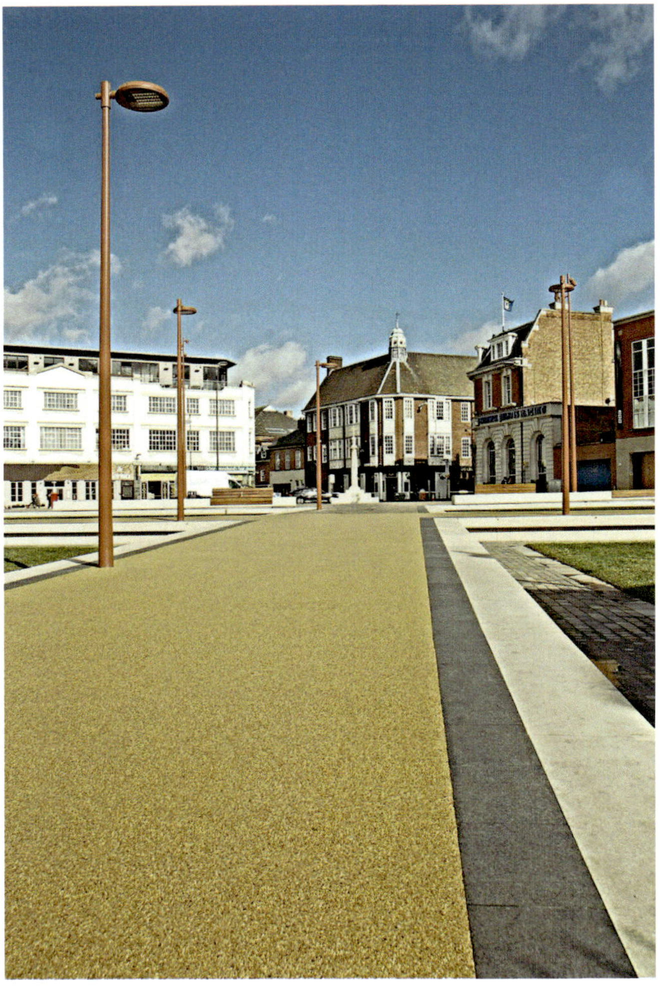

At the heart of medieval Leicester: the view across Jubilee Square towards the ancient High Cross.

Leicester was the birthplace of the academic study of English local history, pioneered by William George Hoskins and supported by Frederick Attenborough, the Principal of what was then University College, Leicester. Initially, Hoskins' surveys of lost villages in Leicestershire were limited to those he could reach by bicycle. That changed when Attenborough offered to drive him to more distant locations and photograph the landscapes they explored together.

Hoskins followed in the footsteps of John Nichols, the author, editor, printer and publisher of the monumental *History and Antiquities of the County of Leicester*. Published over a span of fifteen years, it comprises 4,500 pages in eight large volumes and contains 5.5 million words. In the wake of Nichols, any history of Leicester is likely to be a 'potted' one!

One of the most appealing aspects of Nichols' history is the occasional footnotes, such as when his coachman became intoxicated while waiting outside Gumley Hall for Nichols to finish an extended visit to the Cradock family, or his complaints about the potholes on the road to Kirby Muxloe. More than 200 years have passed since Nichols published his final volume; 200 dramatic years of war and peace, innovation and invention, industrial growth, and political turbulence.

So, here is another history. This is my version, shaped by the events and the people I believe to be most significant in Leicester's past. It will never be your history because your interpretation of past events will differ. There will always be room for another record of past experiences. Yours is just as valid, and together our histories may enrich our understanding of history.

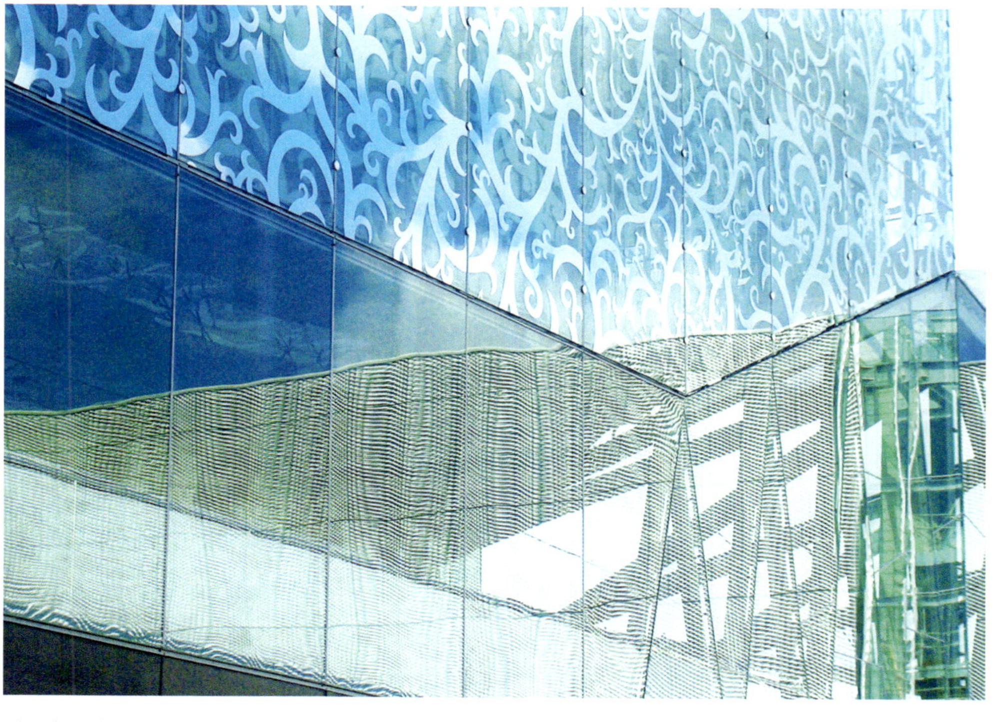

The facade of the John Lewis store: layers of glass with swirling fabric designs acknowledging Leicester's textile-manufacturing history.

I

The Romans and the River

'Veni, Vidi, Vici' – they came, they saw, they conquered – is often attributed to Julius Caesar, though he was not referring to the invasion of Britain. Gradually advancing north from the English Channel, the Roman army in Britain not only faced fierce opposition from native tribes but also a challenging landscape including the major rivers that criss-crossed the island.

For the earliest settlers, rivers held great importance. They were essential for life, providing not only water but also food and transportation. Those who first settled in what is now Leicester followed the well-worn tracks made by wild animals over centuries, descending from higher ground to drink in the shallow water at the river's edge.

For over 2,000 years, the River Soar has played a crucial role in shaping Leicester. Its waters powered the earliest mills, cooled the turbines generating the town's electricity, conveyed sewage away from the town, and served as a conduit for transporting raw materials to factories and manufactured goods to markets. Today, the river is still working for Leicester, serving as a hub for leisure activities, recreation and tourism.

The river's name derives from the linguistic root '-ser', meaning 'to flow'. However, antiquarian scholar William Somner (1598–1669), who compiled the first dictionary of

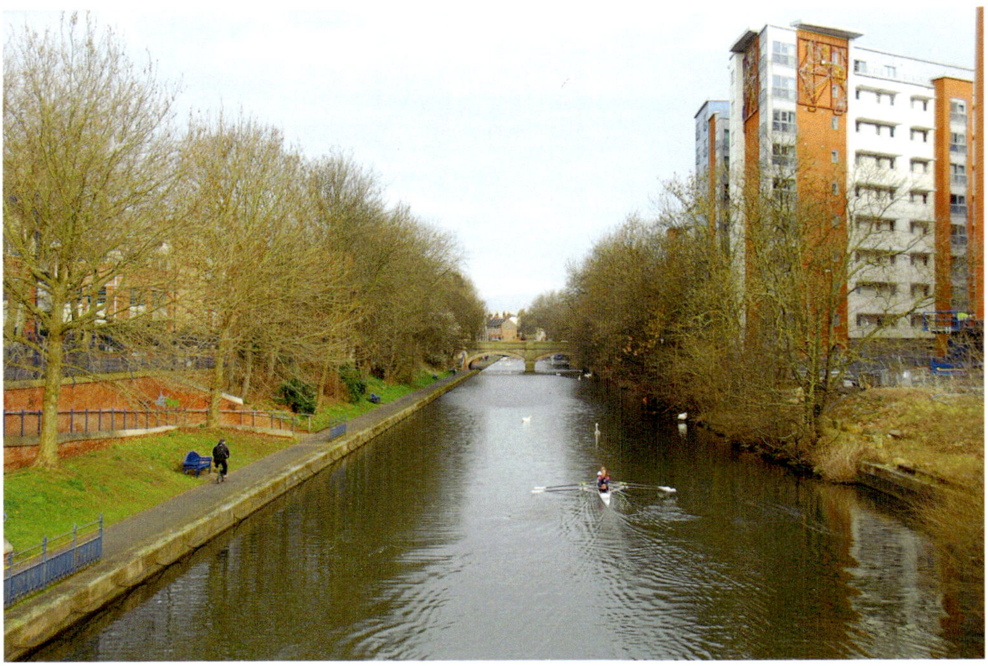

The River Soar 'One Mile Straight' looking towards the Newarke Bridge.

the Anglo-Saxon language, suggested that the river may have originally been called the Leir, from Brittonic *Ligera* or *Ligora*, like the Loire in France. His theory was based on the names of Leicester, Loughborough and the village of Leire, all derived, in his view, from the name of the river.

The earliest inhabitants of Leicester were the Corieltauvi, a tribe spread across the area now known as the East Midlands. Leicester became their capital – hence its early name *Ratae Corieltauvorum*. The Corieltauvi were a loose federation of several independent communities, each with a sense of loyalty to their neighbours. They may have shared similar social practices and, over time, began to recognise the leaders that emerged from the various groups.

By AD 30, the Corieltauvi were minting coins bearing the names of their rulers. This indicates that their society was organised with a written language, a hierarchy of leadership, concepts of property ownership and a monetary structure for trading and accruing wealth. Archaeological evidence confirms that these early Iron Age settlers occupied land on the east bank of the River Soar near the present St Nicholas Circle and Bath Lane.

Volisios is the earliest person known to have had influence over the area. He was clearly a significant figure, although he is known to us only through inscriptions on coins. His name appears on three series of coins minted between around AD 30 and AD 60. Coins found at archaeological digs support the theory that the wider Corieltauvi peoples were led, and governed, by several men. Over time, one man became recognised as the most important member of that group. The name of Volisios is often linked on coins with those of other leaders, including Dumnovellaunus, Dumnocoveros and Cartivellaunos.

Volisios may have become the leader of the Corieltauvi before the Roman invasion and commissioned coinage that included the names of his three lieutenants, each responsible for a specific geographical area of the wider territory. A significant quantity of coins bearing his image has been found in South Yorkshire which suggests that as the Romans advanced from the south, Volisios and a section of the Corieltauvi may have moved from the Leicester area to the north of the region.

It is likely that the Corieltauvi maintained trading links with continental Europe and with the Roman Empire before the Roman invasion. Their trading and the exchange of money for goods may have taken place at the centre of their settlement, creating Leicester's first marketplace. This was close to where the Romans later constructed their forum and near to where a medieval market would later be situated at the High Cross.

The River Soar was also a barrier that restricted the movement of people. A merchant's cart, a centurion's chariot and troops could be taken around a hill, but not around a river. When the Romans arrived and were laying down their important Fosse Way to enable troops and supplies to move swiftly along the northern frontier of their occupation, Leicester became an important crossing point with military barracks to guard it.

In time, the settlement became a strategic hub close to several important military and trade routes. The Fosse Way linked Exeter in the south with Lincoln in the north, and crossed Watling Street at Venonae, or High Cross. Just beyond Venonae to the south was Tripontium, a Roman town of considerable size and status but little known until the work

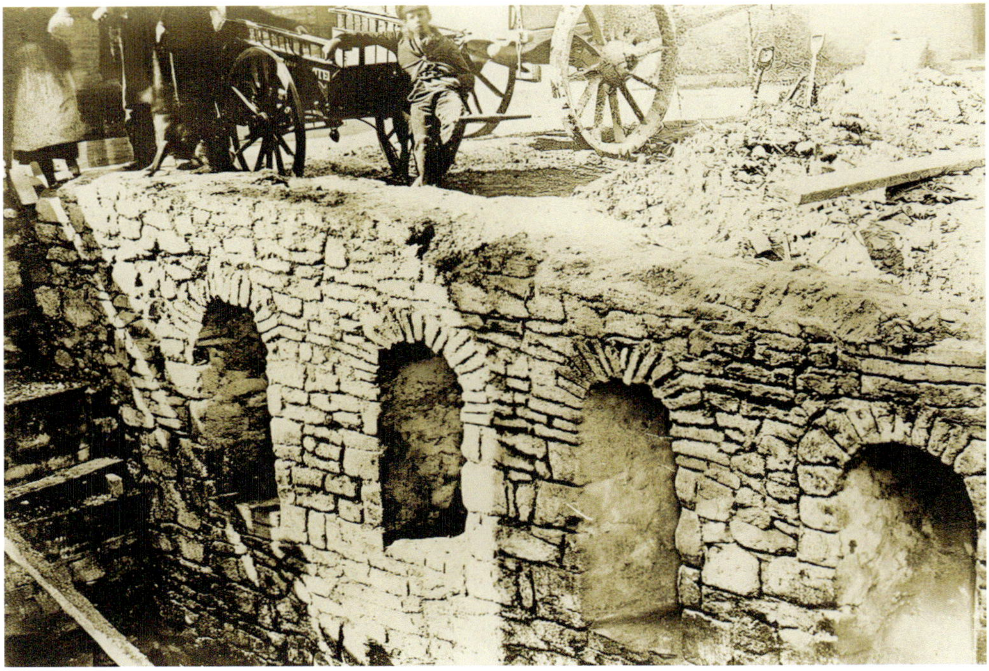

Roman structures dating to the first century AD, the earliest phase of the Roman town, uncovered in Guildhall Lane in 1861.

of antiquarian Matthew Bloxam in 1836. He discovered that, like Leicester, Tripontium had large public baths, an administrative centre and probably also a temple and forum. No doubt the road between Leicester and Tripontium was heavily used, conveying supplies and personnel between the two garrisons.

Venonae was also a significant 'frontier' between the Corieltauvi and Dobunni tribes. The Gartree Road or *Via Devana* linked Colchester in the south-east with Chester in the north-west. At its peak of activity, 500 soldiers of the Ninth Legion were stationed in Leicester to guard this vital intersection.

The North-South Divide

Many of the routes laid down by the Romans have survived and remain an influence not only on the landscape but also the social, economic and even political and religious structure of England. Since the beginning of the Industrial Revolution, economists and politicians have identified a 'north-south' divide.

Sitting, sometimes precariously, on the divide, Leicester was certainly more akin to the north of England during and following the Industrial Revolution, being an industrial city with major iron foundries, boot and shoe and textile industries. North-west Leicestershire was a significant coal-mining area. The railway linking the mines to Leicester was only the third line to be built, following Stockton to Darlington, and Manchester to Liverpool – both firmly in the north. Leicester was the first town in 'the south' to be industrialised by a railway system.

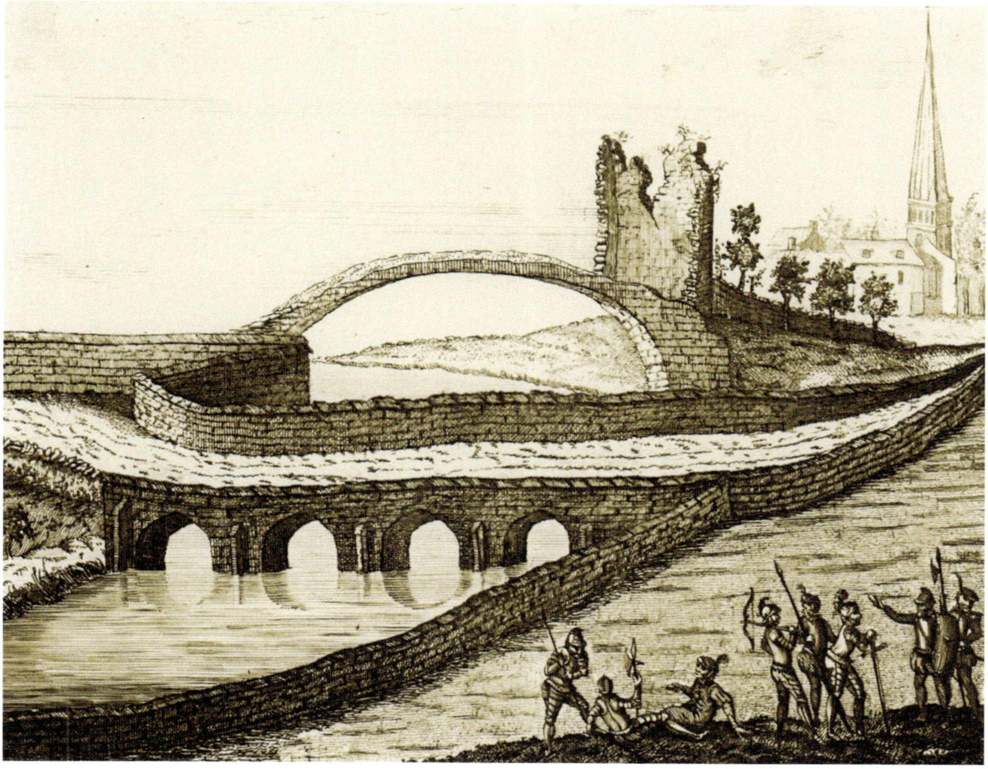

Early crossings of the River Soar at West Bridge, a route since Roman times.

A further fascinating element of the Fosse Way 'divide' in the countryside became evident during the English Civil War and survived until modern times. The road delineated – due to historic land ownership – the supporters of the King (to the south) and the Parliamentarians (to the north). It has been said by at least one church leader in Leicestershire that there was a noticeably 'dour' or 'puritanical' attitude to worship in the parishes on the northern side. To what extent this is real or perceived is a matter for debate, but such ideas demonstrate that the Roman Fosse Way remained an influential physical structure over many centuries.

Verecunda and Lucius

All military garrisons rely on a supply line for food and other necessities. So far from home, the Roman soldiers also needed activities we might now call leisure pursuits. Most of these were provided for in the forum. Leicester's first market traders were there too, as were gladiators imported for the specific purpose of providing entertainment.

Remarkably, we know the names of two of these gladiators. Sometime in the third century, an actress, or a dancer, fell in love with a gladiator by the name of Lucius. Her name was Verecunda, meaning to be shy or modest, or someone who can feel shame, from the verb 'to revere'.

Their feelings for each other were indicated in four words – *VERECVNDA LVDIA LVCIUS GLADIATOR* – scratched around the rim of a broken bowl. The statement was intended to be public knowledge because the young woman turned the fragment of pottery into a necklace to wear around her neck, and the words have survived as one of the earliest written records of personal names from Leicester.

She may have found a street trader to create her amulet, or the pieces of the broken bowl had a more specific significance, perhaps a reminder of a special occasion or a love-token from Lucius on the eve of a contest or following a victory. In any case, the bowl could not be discarded, so the words were etched around the rim, and a friend or street trader drilled a hole through the fragment to enable her to add a thread and wear it with pride.

The fact that her family name can be found further north in the name of a cavalry prefect on Hadrian's Wall prompts many questions, such as how she reached Leicester and why. Pots were used to transport goods as well as for storage, and Samian ware is found throughout the Roman Empire. It was made in many areas of Gaul, France and Germany, so it cannot be assumed, based on the artefact alone, that Verecunda and Lucius were ever in Leicester.

However, this trinket is a personal item of jewellery, and its inscription indicates that it was of great sentimental value to its owner. It would seem very unlikely that this fragment travelled to Leicester separately from its owner, or that Verecunda left the town without it. Verecunda's necklace was rediscovered in 1854 during excavations in Bath Lane in Leicester. Fragments of a first-century glass cup, also from Leicester, have depictions of gladiatorial combat etched upon them, suggesting that such performances took place in the town.

Gladiators in the Roman Empire travelled with their unique form of entertainment from town to town, country to country. Rome did employ female gladiators. It is known that women volunteered for the arena and received training. According to Petronius, writing of the earlier time of Nero, having a female gladiator as part of the spectacle was considered a special treat. Possibly they performed between the main male acts as a kind of lighter entertainment in a similar way to the role of cheerleaders in modern times. Verecunda may have been a female gladiator in her own right, in the same troupe as Lucius, or she may have been a dancer or an actress, or perhaps just a young Leicester girl who fell under the spell of one of the first celebrities to visit the town. Dancers and gladiators represented roles and occupations at the opposite ends of the social spectrum in the Roman Empire.

The Jewry Wall

The Jewry Wall is one of the largest remaining Roman masonry structures in Britain, and the only element of the Roman town to survive above ground. It was built around AD 160 and formed the entrance to the public baths. Bathing was central to Roman life in a communal way. Families, friends and whole communities spent time together, sharing baths and rooms. These complex structures involved rooms heated to different temperatures, and as most Romans bathed daily, merchants and entertainers were also present.

Seneca, the Roman philosopher, gave a vivid description of what life was like living near a town's baths:

> Imagine all kinds of uproar. Fit to make you hate your ears. The hearties are put through their paces, throw their hands about laden with leaden weights, and when they exert themselves, or pretend to, I hear their grunts and their whistling, raucous breathing...

The remains of the Roman baths were discovered by chance in 1936 when a factory was demolished to make way for new swimming baths. The pioneering archaeologist Dame Kathleen Kenyon was commissioned to excavate the site. Before her work, the Jewry Wall was believed to be part of the town's forum, but Kenyon's excavations revealed it was part of a substantial Roman bathing complex. She demonstrated that the Jewry Wall was the west wall of a large, aisled basilica, part of the bath complex. The area included facilities such as the *tepidarium* (warm room), *caldarium* (hot bath), and *frigidarium* (cold bath), which were integral to the social and cultural life of Roman Leicester.

There remains a debate as to how the baths were supplied with water. Although the river was nearby, the baths were constructed on higher ground. Possibly, slaves from Africa or other parts of the Roman Empire were brought in to pump the water, or maybe the curious Rawdykes earthwork was an aqueduct constructed specifically for this purpose. However, it might have been easier for the Roman hydraulic engineers to simply turn the river into a canal rather than build a separate complex structure for the same purpose.

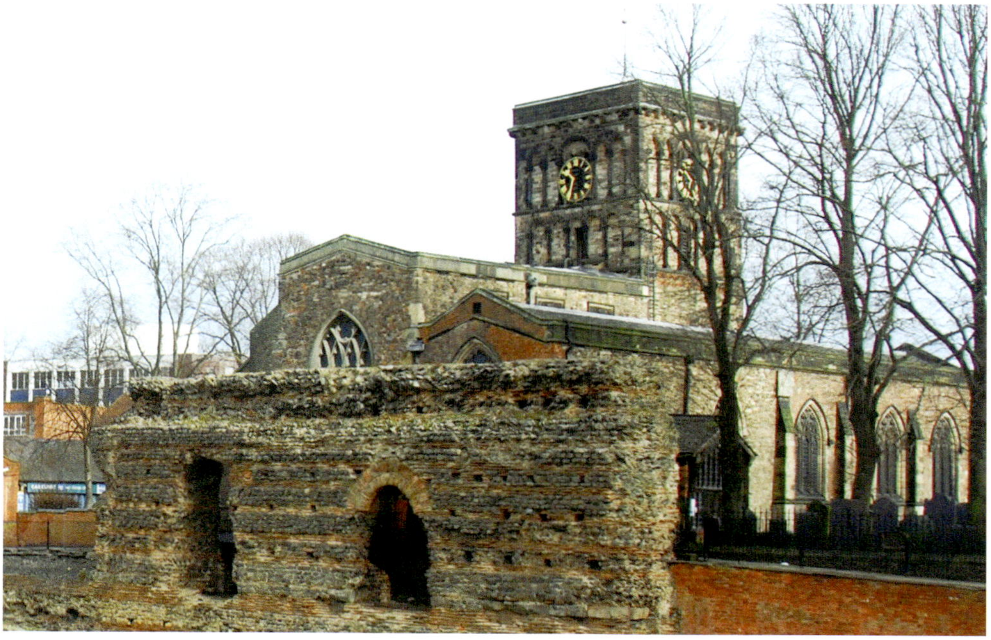

The Jewry Wall and St Nicholas Church.

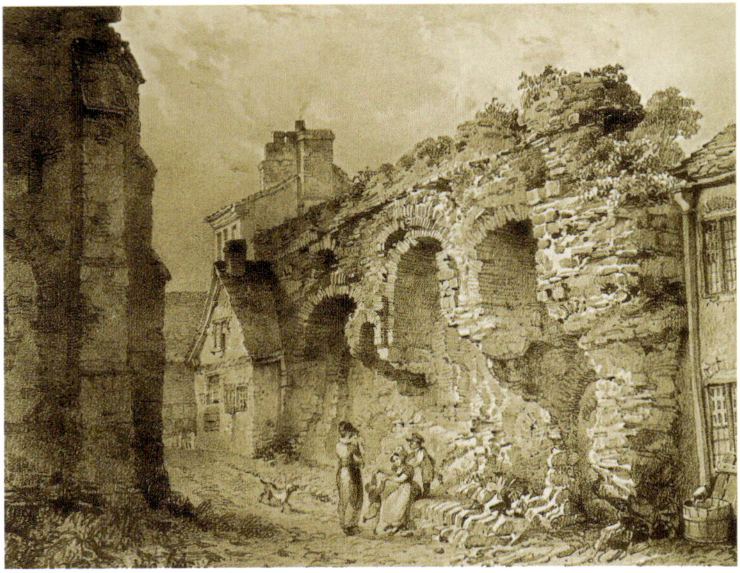

The Jewry Wall with St Nicholas Church in the foreground as recorded by the Leicester architectural artist John Flower in 1826.

Roman Leicester, like Rome itself, developed gradually over time. As in every age, buildings were demolished to make way for new structures as the town grew and gained strategic importance. A market hall and other commercial buildings were constructed, and by the late third century, stone town walls had been added to the earlier earth ramparts and wooden palisades. Fine villas grew up in the surrounding countryside for the wealthier families. The future town and city of Leicester was busy and bustling.

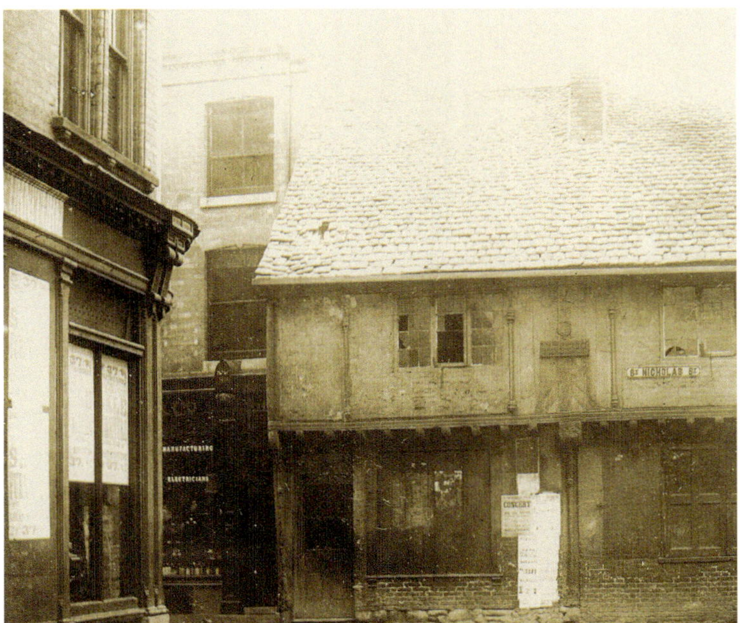

A fine Roman mosaic was discovered beneath this shop in former St Nicholas Street.

2

What Happened Next?

The textbooks state that the Romans left Britain soon after AD 400 to support the fight to defend their homeland. Rome was under attack and their empire was under threat. However, there is an inherent danger in narrating history only in terms of events or dates.

The Romans had occupied Britain for 350 years, equivalent to six or more generations. Those Romans who left our shores were probably very different in outlook and experience from that of their ancestors, as different as we are from our great-great-great-great grandparents. Over the past four centuries we have experienced an ever-increasing rate of change brought about by the Industrial Revolution and scientific discoveries. The rate of change following the ending of the Roman occupation may have been slower but nonetheless equally disruptive for those who lived through it in the town of Leicester.

Some of Roman descent did not leave. Why should they? Having been born here and inherited family homes and possessions, these descendants of the original legionaries who took Leicester understandably saw Leicester and the surrounding area as their home. Being of mixed race over several generations, some must have felt little or no affinity with Rome. Others may have experienced split loyalties, even bitterness.

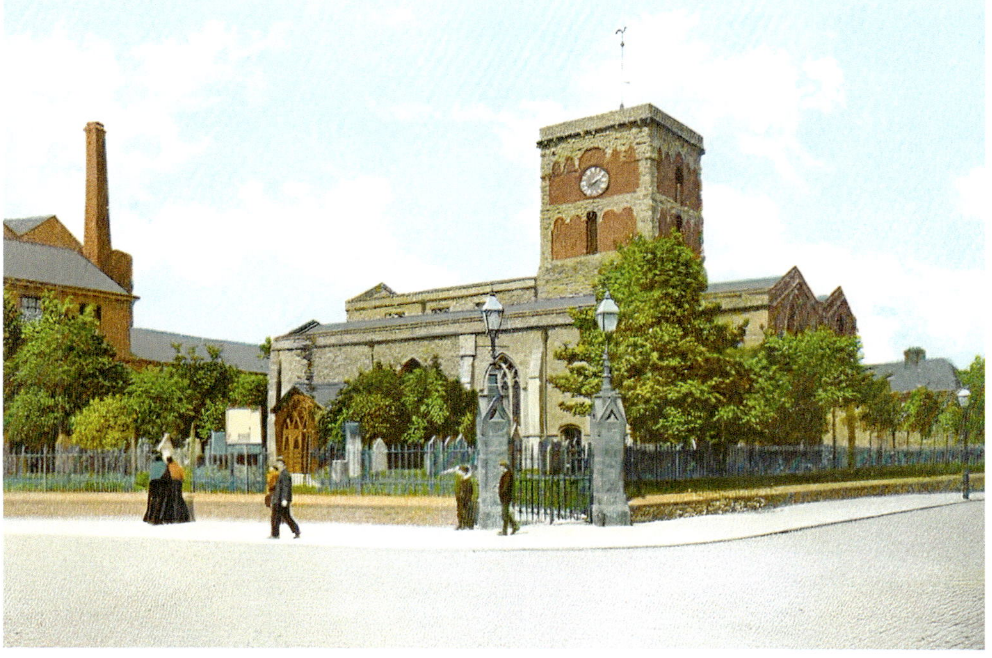

St Nicholas Church, pictured here in Edwardian times, was probably built on the site of an earlier religious structure.

Honorius, the Roman Emperor, sent a 'goodbye letter'. Paraphrased, he wrote, 'fight bravely and defend your lives ... you are on your own now.' He was addressing those children of former legionaries as well as the Britons, but it was not a case of 'all change' just because the Roman Emperor has issued a decree.

What happened next in Leicester has long been a matter for debate. The 'Dark Ages' is a useful label for a time in history with minimal physical evidence to confirm what really happened, although archaeology is now steadily shining a light through that darkness.

Continuity or Discontinuity?

An interesting element of any history is continuity, or the lack of it. After the departure of the Romans, can we assume that Leicester was deserted, and the buildings left to crumble or to be robbed of their stone? Or was Leicester still occupied by remnants of the previous community. If so, was this remnant a cohesive community, or a lawless one? We know from many later events in history that social turbulence and unrest in a country or region often follows the withdrawal of a power that has previously rigorously enforced order and law.

Some historians have suggested that the change in the name of the settlement we now know as Leicester indicates a lack of continuity and points to a period after the departure of the Romans when the town was deserted. They note that by the time of the Domesday Book, the Roman name *Ratae Corietauvorum* had been replaced by *Ledecestre*. However, Leicester derives from the Old English *Ligoraceastre* or *Lægreceastre*, which in turn may come from 'city on the Ligore', possibly a previous name for the River Soar. It could also be derived from 'City of the Legions'.

The earliest recorded name for Leicester, written in Ptolemy's *Geographia* (*c.* AD 150), was *Ratae*, thought to be a Romanised Celtic (British) word meaning 'ramparts'. Later in the Roman period it became *Ratae Corieltavorum*, and it was still described as *Rate Corion Eltauori* in the early eighth century. By the end of that century something had changed, and it had come to be known as *Legorensis Civitatis*. It wasn't known as *Leircestre* until after the eleventh century.

Although we cannot be certain whether Leicester was lived in during the ensuing centuries, the Roman occupation left its mark, not only through dominant physical structures such as the Jewry Wall but also on the social fabric of the town and countryside. There was certainly some continuity in the form of the Roman street plan. The layout constructed by the Romans can still be seen. Even today, after 2,000 years of change and decades of town planning, motorists in Leicester drive through road junctions and crossroads close to the intersections of the Roman street plan.

The junction of the modern St Nicholas Place and Guildhall Lane is very close to where the Fosse Way once crossed the main north-to-south street at the heart of the Roman town. Not far away, until some years ago, a shallow depression stretched across Sanvey Gate just before the junction with St Margaret's Way, the last remnants of the former town ditch. Passengers on buses could feel the jolt, although they may not have understood its significance.

Of course, we are conjecturing what might have happened in Leicester over a period longer than the Roman occupation. It is a fascinating thought that the 'dark ages' covered around 500 years and in the region of twenty generations. The people who witnessed the Norman invasion in 1066 were far removed in their experiences and social environment from their predecessors who saw the Romans arrive, and who knows from whom they may have descended? Could there have been a continuity of stories and legends passed on from generation to generation? Or in those post-Roman turbulent times, were the stories lost because of the mass upheaval of people across the region?

We must acknowledge the work of a Benedictine monk known as the Venerable Bede who recorded so much of the history of this time. He completed his *Ecclesiastical History of the English* in AD 731. Unfortunately, a lot of the details in his writings are wrong. However, we have another very informative source in the form of Gildas, a British monk, who wrote *The Ruin of Britain*, the only near-contemporary source for the collapse of Roman Britain and the arrival of the Anglo-Saxons.

Gildas was a British historian who founded a monastic house in Brittany known after him as the monastery of St Gildas de Rhuys. Gildas was born in Britain, possibly in what is now Scotland or northern England, though some traditions place his birth in Wales. His writings suggest he was familiar with events in southern Britain such as the Saxon invasions and the state of the British church. His writings reflect a distinctly unfavourable opinion of the British rulers of that era.

His *De Excidio et Conquestu Britanniae* ('On the Ruin and Conquest of Britain') is one of the few sources for the history of England for the centuries following the departure of the Romans. Gildas regarded the events that followed, or at least those he heard about, as God's punishment for the sins of the Britons, though the sins of the Romans were not addressed.

Not long after the Romans departed, Britain was threatened by invaders from the north. Without the military defences of the Romans, Britain was an open door.

The native Britons called upon Germanic tribes including the Angles, Saxons and Jutes to help defend their land. Bede noted that the Angles, before coming to Great Britain, 'dwelt in a land called Angulus which lies between the province of the Jutes and the Saxons and remains unpopulated to this day.' Unfortunately, these 'allies' were not to be trusted. They eventually turned against the native population and began to settle across the country, establishing three principal kingdoms, Northumbria, Wessex and Mercia, the latter centred on the River Trent and its tributaries, in what might now be loosely described as the Midlands. Was this when the template for a multi-racial England began? Certainly, the English language reflects these arrivals and their increasing influence on the societies that developed.

Dark Earth

Whilst investigating the 'dark ages', researchers and archaeologists often encounter dark earth, a layer of material found lying above the remains of early structures. It is very similar to what gardeners describe as compost. Dark earth clearly indicates previous human occupation but the process by which it was formed has given rise to various theories and conjecture. Garden compost is one suggestion. Another is that it is the result of the gradual composting of refuse tipped on the land. It may also be the decomposed remains of wooden structures and thatch.

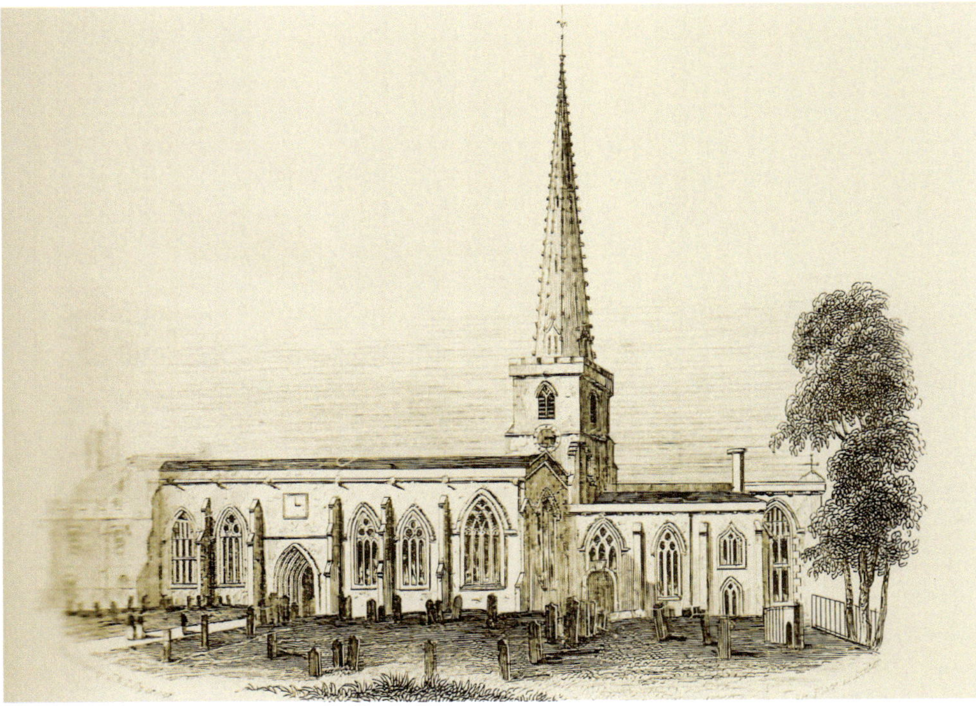

St Martin's Church, later Leicester Cathedral, from John Nichols' *History & Antiquities of the County of Leicester,* 1815.

Dark earth is significant in several respects, including how it shows that ground levels in places of habitation have changed since the time of the Romans. A good example of this change in ground levels can be seen at the rear of the BBC studios at 9 St Nicholas Place opposite the Guildhall. Beneath the studios and extending under the courtyard that opens out into Guildhall Lane is a rectangular stone room or undercroft. The floor level is at least 5 metres below the floor of the modern building. Along the wall on the western side of the structure are several recesses lined with Roman bricks. It has been suggested that these were windows that opened out into a courtyard which may have extended towards Highcross Street.

The Kingdom of Mercia

The name *Mercia* comes from Old English and means 'boundary folk' or 'people of the borderlands'. It derives from the Old English word *Mierce,* which is related to *mearc,* meaning 'boundary' or 'border'. It reflects its geographical position, originally on the frontier between Anglo-Saxon settlers and the native Britons.

Hence the role of Leicester as a significant border settlement continued, and possibly remains to this day. Does the 'East Midlands' have a cultural identity of its own? Does Leicester identify more with cities to the north like Nottingham, or with those to the south such as Northampton? Is the perceived boundary the modern A5 to the south or the A46 to the north?

Mercia converted to Christianity in the mid-seventh century under King Peada. The Diocese of Mercia was established in AD 656, later becoming the Diocese of Lichfield. In addition to Lichfield, Tamworth was an administrative centre for Mercia.

Vikings, Danes and the Danelaw

History tells of the 'Viking Age' and the 'Danelaw' and often appears to refer to both Vikings and Danes without distinction or qualification. Simply put, the term 'Viking' refers to all seafaring people from Scandinavia including Denmark, Norway and Sweden. The Danes refer specifically to the North Germanic tribe that inhabited southern Scandinavia at that time.

It is commonly agreed that the Viking Age began with the raiding of the abbey on Lindisfarne in AD 793. Accounts describe it as a savage attack, as were other early raids. The monastery at Lindisfarne was one of the main centres of Christianity in the kingdom of Northumbria and the assault sent tremors throughout the whole of English Christendom.

The Anglo-Saxon Chronicle recorded the event in these words:

> Here were dreadful forewarnings come over the land of Northumbria, and woefully terrified the people: these were amazing sheets of lightning and whirlwinds, and fiery dragons were seen flying in the sky. A great famine soon followed these signs, and shortly after in the same year, on the sixth day before the ides of January, the woeful inroads of heathen men destroyed God's church in Lindisfarne island by fierce robbery and slaughter.

The twelfth-century chronicle *Historia Regum* (*History of Kings*), written, it is thought, by Simeon, a Benedictine monk at Durham Cathedral, recorded that the invaders 'laid everything waste with grievous plundering, trampled the holy places with polluted steps, dug up the altars and seized all the treasures of the holy church'. He describes how the invaders dragged many of the brothers of the monastery away in chains and drowned others in the sea.

Events such as these understandably gave the Vikings notoriety as pirates, but they were also explorers, travelling as far as the Mediterranean, North Africa, the Middle East and even North America, establishing trade routes. Many Vikings were fishermen, farmers, craftsmen and traders in their home countries.

Hollywood has tended to portray the Vikings as filthy and unkempt – like certain fictional species encountered by Captain James Kirk and his successors during the voyages of the Starship Enterprise – and they did not wear horned helmets.

Most relevant to the history of Leicester is that during the late ninth to eleventh centuries the Vikings occupied a large area of England including the five boroughs of Derby, Leicester, Lincoln, Nottingham and Stamford, establishing Danish law and culture. This area became known as the Danelaw, a region where Danish laws and customs dominated. Again, Leicester was near the border zone between the Danelaw and Saxon Mercia.

So how were the people of Leicester affected by these dramatic events of international significance? Did they even notice? Is it likely that these wider events were also echoed on the doorsteps of the inhabitants of the town? By AD 877 the Danes had occupied Leicester. In AD 918 the Saxons recaptured the town.

We can also turn to familiar Leicester street names for clues. In Old Norse, the suffix 'gata' means a way, path or road. So we have Humberstone Gate and Belgrave Gate, the way or route to those villages, and Gallowtree Gate, the route to the gallows, as well as Churchgate, the way to St Margaret's Church. All running along or exiting and entering on the eastern boundary of the medieval town.

Medieval tradition suggests that St Margaret's Church was the mother church of the borough and one of the oldest places of Christian worship in England, dating back to AD 679, coincidentally the probable date when King Æthelred of Mercia married Princess Osthryth, the sister of King Ecgfrith of Northumbria. It is the only ancient Leicester church located outside the former Roman walls.

Certainly, village names in Leicestershire, such as Frisby, Hoby, Rotherby, Brooksby and Rearsby, are Danish in origin, showing that they settled along the terraces that bordered the valley of the River Wreake. The word 'Wreake' is an Old Norse word describing the river as tortuous and twisting. The Saxons were above them (at least in altitude) occupying the higher land. An interesting situation can be found in the modern settlement of Smeeton Westerby which connects Saxon Smeeton and Danish Westerby, and where the centre of both settlements, now one village, can still be seen. Two communities with very different cultural ancestries that appear to have been able to live side-by-side.

England continued to be dominated by different powers and influences. It was an unstable period which precipitated the Norman invasion of 1066. Once again, the country was vulnerable to attack.

3

And then the Normans

The establishment of Norman rule changed Leicester for ever in terms of the layout of the town, the buildings, including churches, and even the political governance.

The telling of history tends to be divided into landmark events set in chronological order; but this approach can be misleading because it draws attention to certain events with the consequence that other events seem less significant.

This certainly applies to the Norman Invasion of 1066, because to understand why it happened, it must be seen in the context of what had previously taken place in Britain since the departure of the Romans. The conquest was the result of a series of events that began in the reign of Edward the Confessor, last king of the Anglo-Saxon royal line. Edward had no children and used the lack of an heir to play off those who wanted to acquire the throne. These included Harold Godwineson, later Harold II, the powerful earl of Wessex, Tostig, Harold's exiled brother, and Harald III Hardraade, king of Norway.

On his deathbed, Edward named Harold as his successor. He was crowned the following day, but his right to the succession was compromised because he had previously sworn an oath, in William of Normandy's presence, to defend William's right to the throne.

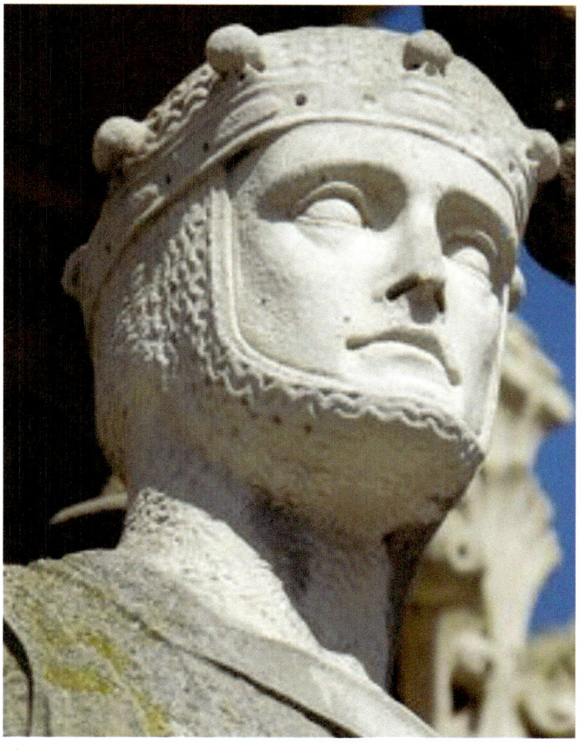

The statute of Simon de Montfort, 6th Earl of Leicester, on the city's iconic Haymarket Memorial Clock Tower.

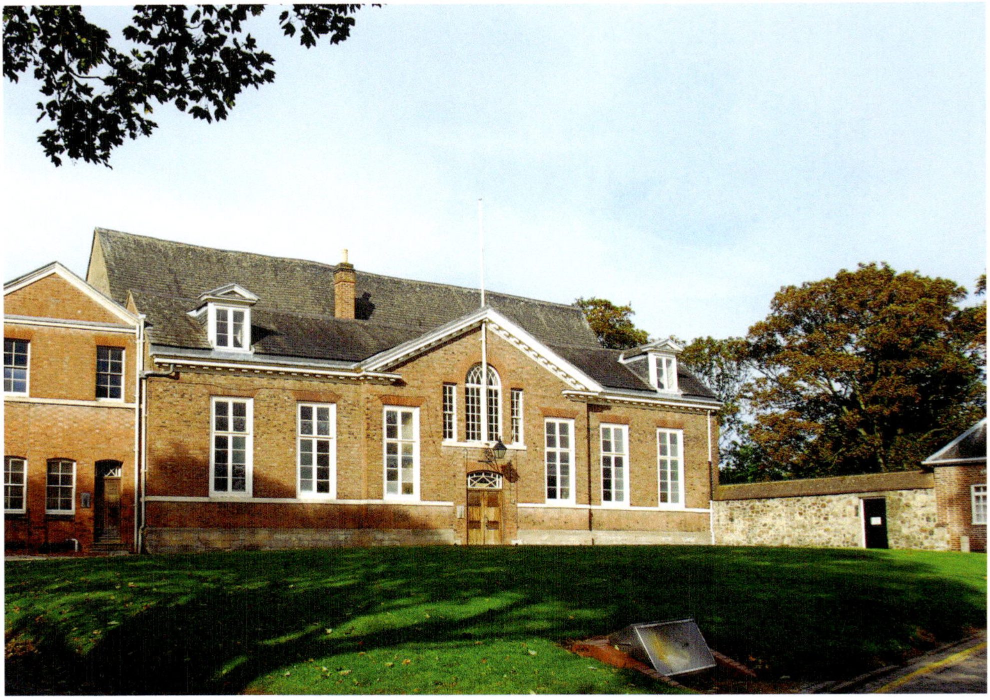

Leicester Castle, now the home of De Montfort University's Business School.

The spring and summer of 1066 were tough for Harold. Tostig began raiding the southern and eastern coasts of England, eventually joining forces with Harald III. Harold was forced to dismiss his army in September because he ran out of supplies and the peasant soldiers needed to go home to their fields for the harvest. The south of the country was consequently left without defences. Harald II and Tostig then invaded from the north, drawing Harold's remaining militia away from the south. Harold won a decisive victory at Stamford Bridge in Yorkshire on 25 September, in which both Harald III and Tostig were killed.

With immaculate strategic timing, William of Normandy's fleet set sail just two days later, and on 28 September landed at Pevensey Bay, north-east of Beachy Head and less than 13 miles' march along the coast from Hastings.

William allowed the Anglo-Saxon Earls of Mercia to keep their lands because they did not fight against him at Hastings on condition that they accepted William's authority as king and as their feudal lord.

Hugh de Grandmesnil

The Grandmesnil family achieved prominence in around 1050 in Normandy where the family became rich and famous for breeding and training war horses. After the Conquest, William rewarded Hugh for his loyalty and service, and for fighting beside him at Hastings, by giving him 100 manors, sixty-five of them in Leicestershire. He was also appointed Sheriff of Leicestershire.

By the time of the Domesday Survey, a castle had been built which William later handed over to Hugh de Grandmesnil, and at some time it was rebuilt in stone. The Survey notes that Hugh owned no fewer than 190 of the 322 houses in the borough. The king himself owned thirty-nine, and more jointly with Hugh. The Survey suggests that by this time, Leicester was thriving as a town with 322 houses and six churches. The population was probably between around 1,500 and 2,000.

After William's death, seemingly inevitable family squabbles followed. The winner was William the Conqueror's third son, William Rufus. The historian Frank Barlow described this William as a 'rumbustious, devil-may-care soldier, without natural dignity or social graces, with no cultivated tastes and little show of conventional religious piety or morality – indeed, according to his critics, addicted to every kind of vice'.

Unfortunately for Leicester, Hugh de Grandmesnil backed the wrong horse in the succession race, and William Rufus took revenge by confiscating the castle and having part of the town destroyed. Later, Hugh apparently made amends, and his authority, lands and property were restored to him.

As with the Romans, the Normans brought order to the town by imposing rigid civic administration. As Leicester became more organised as a society, the population grew and trades, including the production of woollen and leather goods, developed. In the centuries that followed – the so-called Middle Ages – that initial Norman influence permeated every aspect of life for Leicester people, the markets, merchants, businessmen, religion and civic administration.

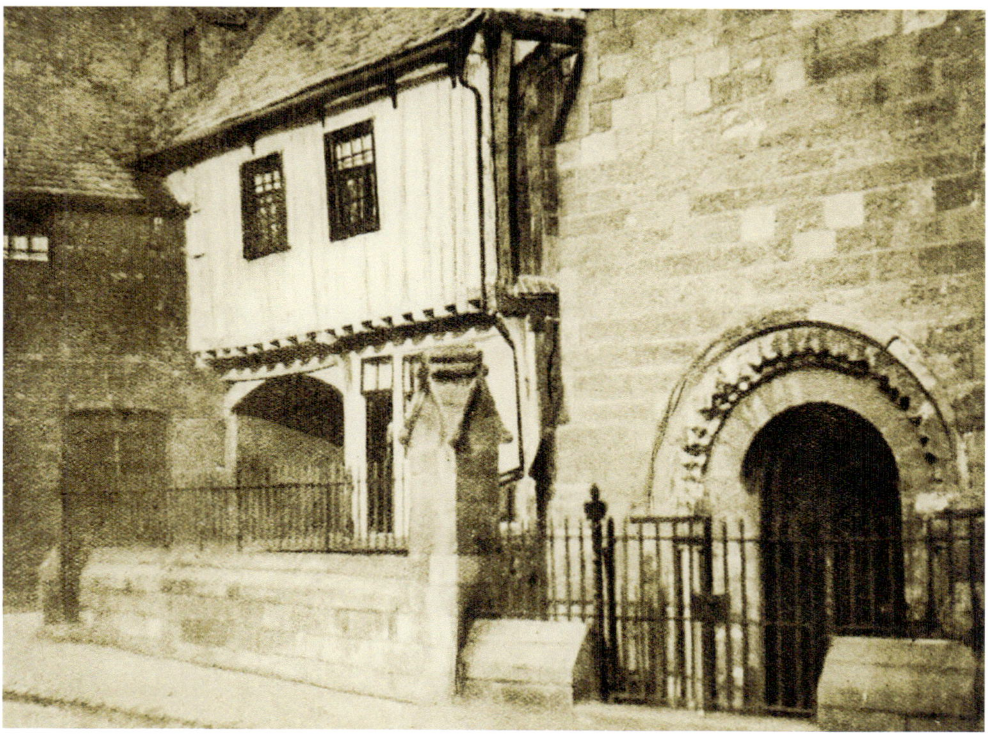

The medieval Castle Yard gatehouse and the Norman-styled doorway in St Mary de Castro.

After the death of Hugh de Grandmesnil in 1098, the succession of Norman lords in Leicester followed a somewhat fragmented path, influenced by both inheritance and royal favour. Hugh's eldest son inherited his father's lands. Control of the honour of Leicester passed into the Beaumont family through marriage alliances and royal grants. Robert Blanchmains, the 3rd Earl of Leicester (*c.* 1130–90), was a key figure in the 1174 rebellion against Henry II which led to the destruction of parts of Leicester Castle. By the thirteenth century, Leicester was firmly under the control of the Earls of Leicester, who were closely tied to the royal family. Eventually, the honour of Leicester became part of the Duchy of Lancaster, and after 1399, it was absorbed into the Crown when Henry Bolingbroke, Duke of Lancaster, became King Henry IV.

The Honour of Leicester

Following the Norman Conquest, an honour referred to a collection of estates held by a single lord, often spread across multiple counties. These honours operated as semi-autonomous administrative and judicial units, complete with their own courts, officials and obligations to the Crown.

The Honour of Leicester was one of the largest and most strategically important of these feudal lordships. It covered an extensive network of estates and manorial holdings, all centred on the town and castle of Leicester. Established in the late eleventh century, it was originally based on lands granted to Hugh de Grandmesnil. The honour expanded significantly in the twelfth century, particularly after the unification of the Grandmesnil and Beaumont estates, which allowed the Earls of Leicester to consolidate their power.

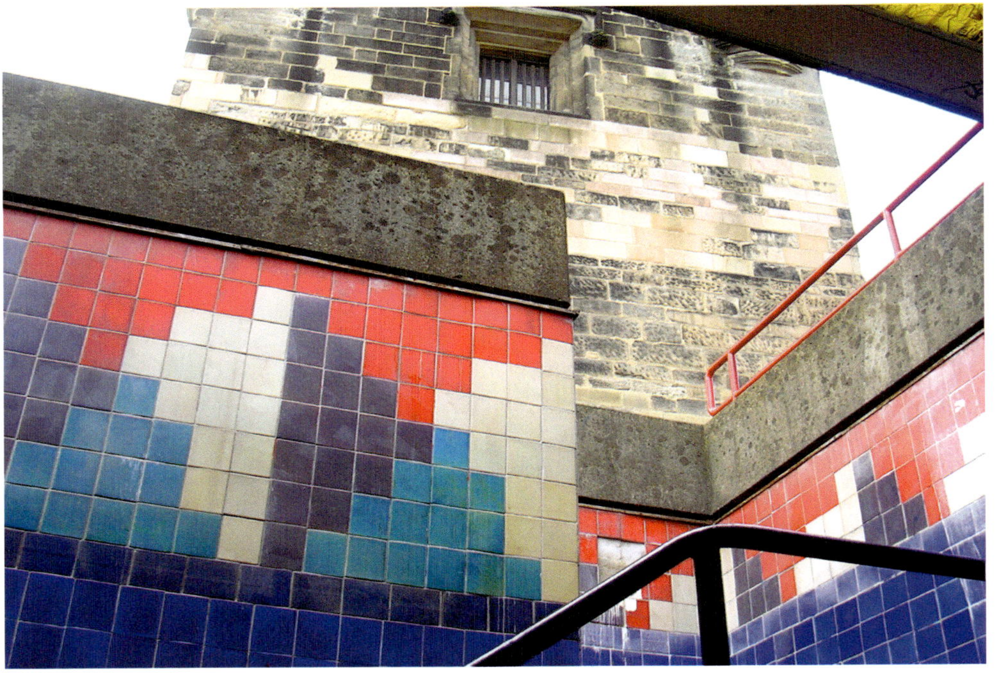

Part of the former mosaic-themed 1970s development of Magazine Square next to the Newarke (Magazine) Gateway.

The honour maintained its own stewardship, courts and military obligations, and its lords exercised a near-regal authority within their domain, including the rights to administer justice and collect taxes.

The Sacking of Leicester

Shortly after Easter in 1173, Henry the Young King, the eldest son of King Henry II, rose in rebellion against his father, plunging the Plantagenet realms of England and France into turmoil. Among his most prominent allies was Robert Blanchmains, 3rd Earl of Leicester, whose support for the uprising would bring devastating consequences to the town of Leicester and its people.

In retaliation for Blanchmains' attacks on royal forces in Normandy, King Henry II dispatched his Chief Justiciar, Richard de Lucy, to seize Leicester. On 3 July, de Lucy arrived with the so-called 'Army of England' and laid siege to the town. Accompanying the troops were nearly 200 carpenters, tasked with constructing siege engines to breach Leicester's defences.

For three weeks, the town withstood the assault. But disaster struck when a fire swept through Leicester, forcing the rebel garrison – led by Ansketil Mallory – to retreat into the safety of the castle. With their protectors gone, the townspeople were left vulnerable, and surrendered on 28 July.

The rebellion continued until the summer of 1174, when King Henry II finally crushed the remaining resistance. Leicester Castle was among the last rebel strongholds to fall. In the aftermath, parts of the castle and the town's defences were deliberately destroyed to prevent Leicester from ever again serving as a base for rebellion.

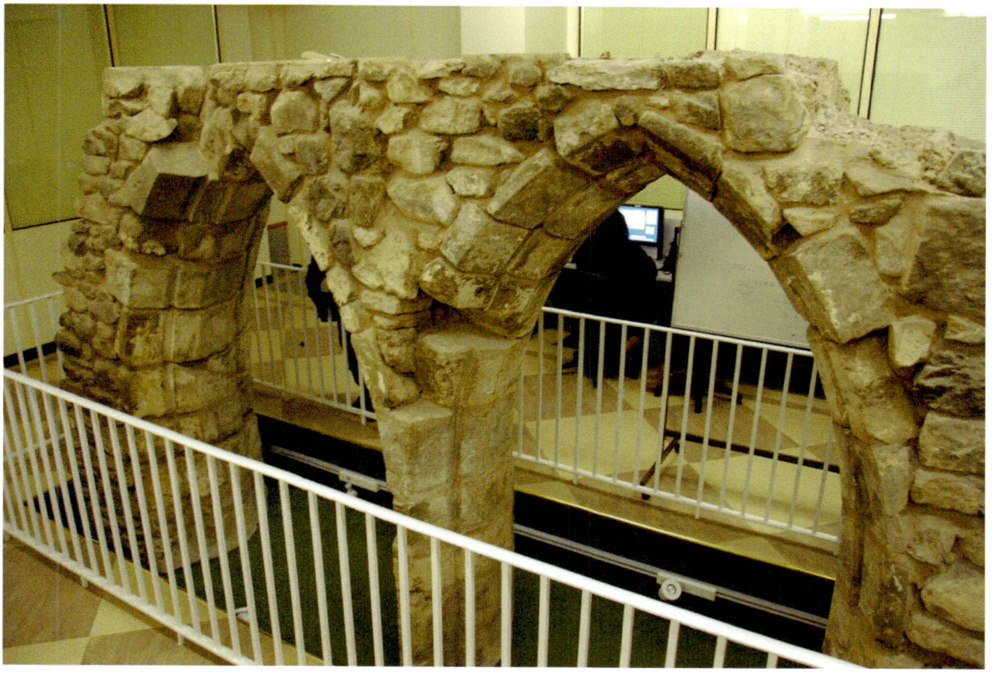

The remaining arches of the former Church of the Annunciation of Our Lady of the Newarke in Leicester, founded in 1353 by Henry of Grosmont, 1st Duke of Lancaster.

St Mary de Castro

The parish and collegiate church of St Mary de Castro is at the heart of Leicester's history and is a fine example of Norman influence on the character of Leicester. The children of Alfred the Great, Edward the Elder and his sister, Æthelflæd, are said to have founded the first church on the site in 918. After the Conquest, it was demolished by Hugh de Grandmesnil who commissioned a new church on the earlier Saxon foundations. There followed several rebuilds and modifications. In 1107, Robert de Beaumont, Earl of Leicester, rebuilt and extended the nave by adding the sanctuary.

The church and the castle were rebuilt again after the sacking of the town in 1173. The chancel was lengthened and the Norman sedilia in the south wall was moved. The nave was heightened by the introduction of the clerestory above the Norman windows and a freestanding tower was built in the thirteenth century.

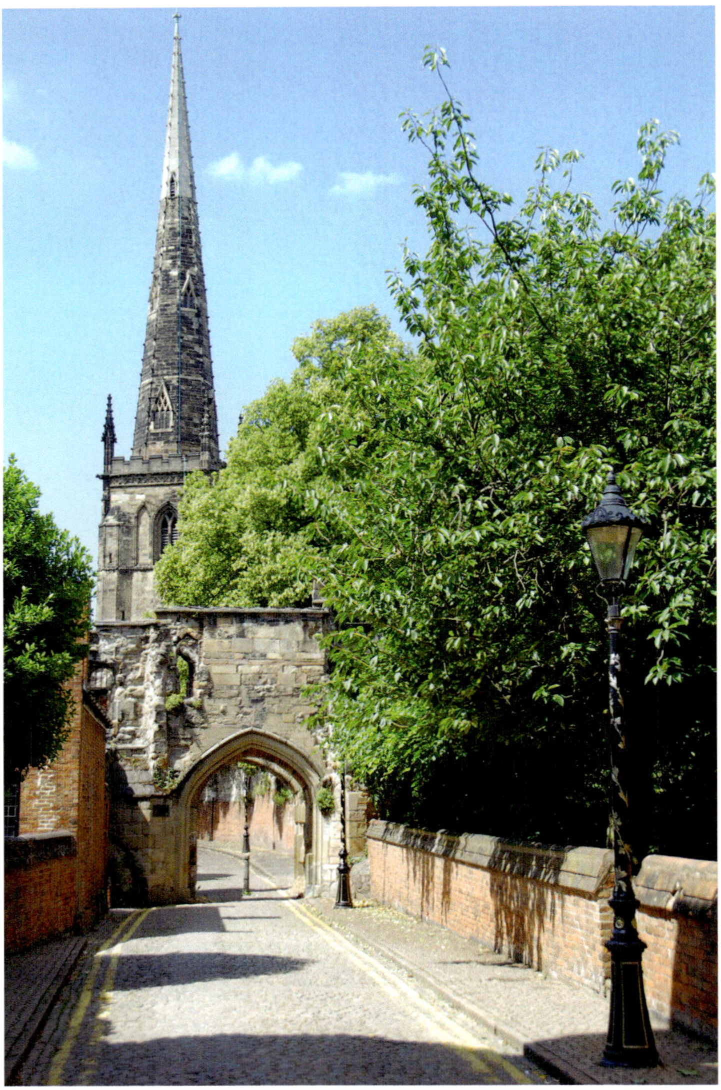

The fourteenth-century Turret Gateway and Castle View before the spire of St Mary de Castro was removed.

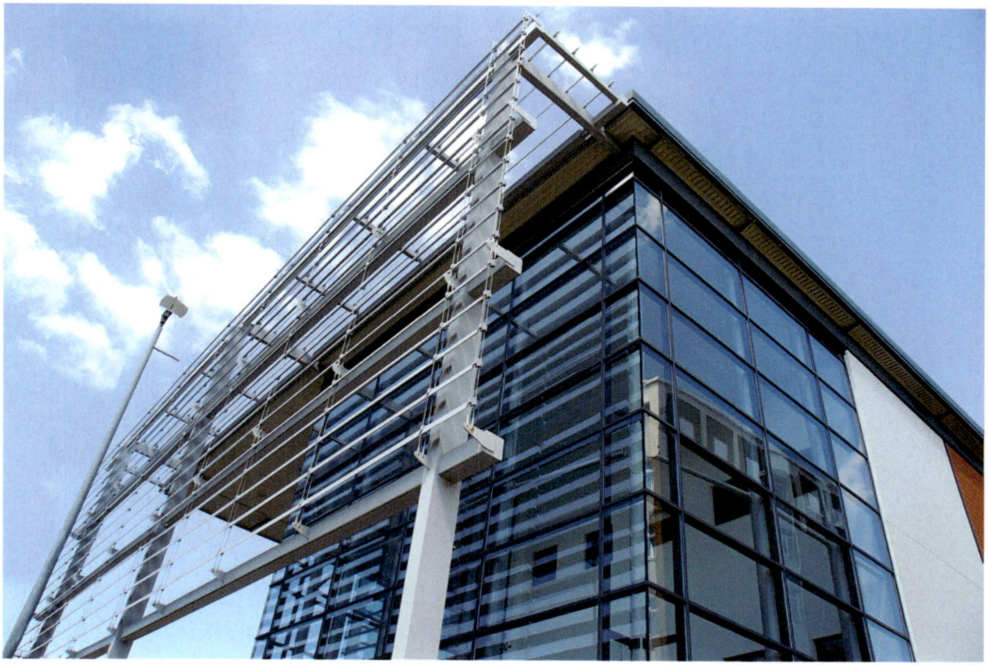

De Montfort University's Student Union building in the Newarke.

Many historical events of national significance have taken place within the walls of St Mary de Castro. In 1201, a meeting of discontented barons took place at Leicester Castle. These barons are believed to have attended services at St Mary de Castro, linking the church to the early events that led to the Magna Carta.

It is widely believed, though not definitively proven, that Geoffrey Chaucer married Philippa (de) Roet at St Mary de Castro in Leicester in around 1366. Philippa was a lady-in-waiting to Queen Philippa of Hainault, and the sister of Katherine Swynford, who later became the third wife of John of Gaunt, Chaucer's patron and close associate. This connection to the royal court and to Leicester through John of Gaunt strengthens the likelihood of the marriage taking place at this church, which was within the precincts of Leicester Castle.

The Parliament of Bats was a session of the English Parliament held in Leicester in 1426 during the minority of King Henry VI, who was still an infant at the time. The name stems from the unusual weapons carried by attendees. Due to intense political tensions, especially between Cardinal Henry Beaufort (the Bishop of Winchester) and Humphrey, Duke of Gloucester (the king's uncle and Lord Protector), swords were banned from the meeting. Instead, many nobles and their retainers came armed with clubs or 'bats'. The Parliament met in the Great Hall of Leicester Castle, and during the Parliament, the young Henry VI was knighted at the nearby church of St Mary de Castro.

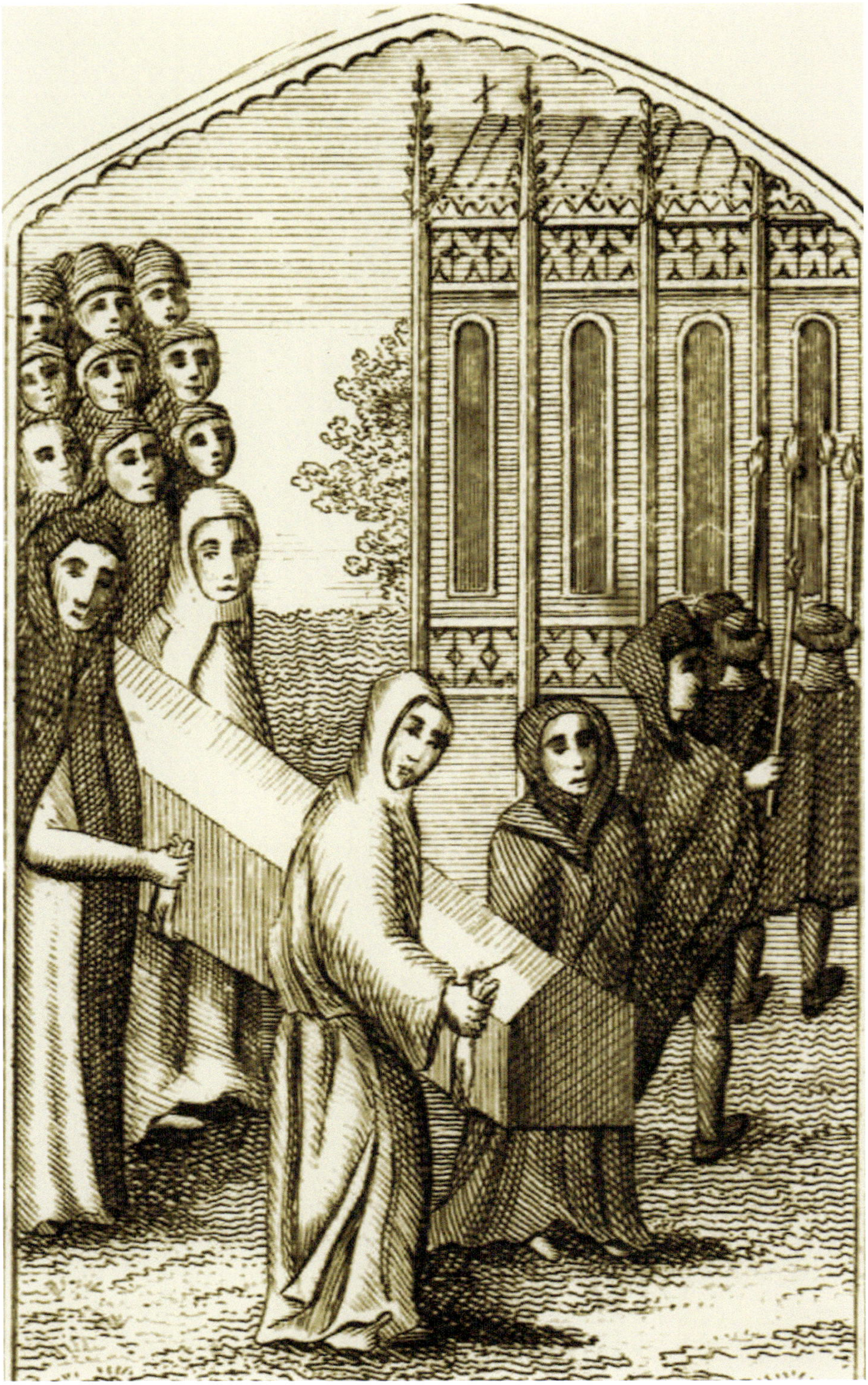

A burial in Greyfriars depicted in Nichol's *History of Leicester*. Could this refer to the burial of Richard III?

4

Churches, Hospitals, Abbeys and Friaries

A walk through Leicester in the Middle Ages would have involved an encounter with numerous religious buildings, from parish churches to monastic houses. Around almost every corner of the town another place of worship would come into view, or one would pass a priest in surplice or a monk in his habit.

The endowment of hospitals, churches and monastic communities after the Conquest served several purposes for the Norman rulers. It enabled them to demonstrate their authority and legitimise their rule, as well as gaining favour with the Church. For some it was seen as atonement for sins and to secure salvation. Nobles and kings endowed monasteries and hospitals as acts of piety and to ensure prayers for their souls.

Many of the locations in Leicester have survived as modern placenames, even where the original buildings no longer exist. Greyfriars is an obvious example which is more familiar now to residents and visitors alike since the discovery and reinterment of the body of Richard III in 2012. St Peter's Lane is less well-known, now tucked in between the Highcross Centre and Churchgate, and there was once a St Clement's Lane near to All Saints' Church.

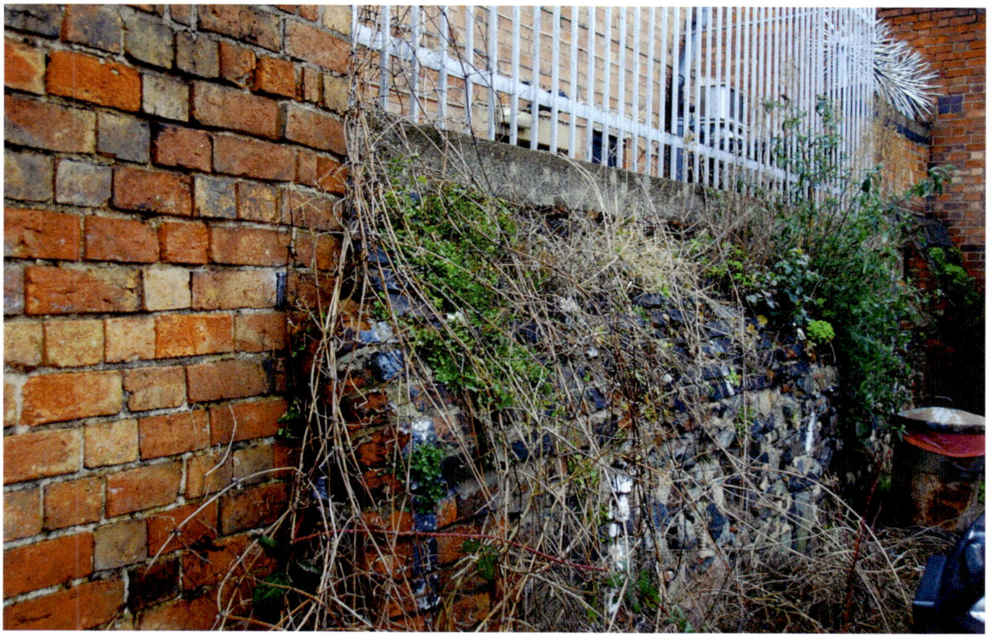

A surviving fragment of a wall believed to be part of the Greyfriars church, in a car park off New Street.

Greyfriars

There are three major milestones in the history of Greyfriars: the founding, the Battle of Bosworth and the discovery, in September 2012, of the body of King Richard III in its precincts.

Working back in time, a belief that had gained significant credibility over the centuries was that the body of Richard III had been removed from its first resting place and dumped in the River Soar. It stems from a legend that, as Richard and his men left Leicester across the West Bridge en route to Bosworth Field on that fateful day in 1485, his spurs scraped against the parapet, prompting an 'old crone' to point a long figure at the King and to prophesy (no doubt in a cackling voice) that it would be the monarch's head that would be scraping in the same place on his return, his body presumably slumped over a horse.

Logically, this scenario seemed unlikely. Henry VII, the victor at Bosworth, ensured that the body of Richard was seen by the people of the town to convince them of his victory. Having allowed the body to lie in state for three days, and then to be given a decent burial, why should Henry, the first Tudor monarch, revive old rivalries and loyalties by insisting that Richard's body is exhumed and publicly thrown into the river? Surely, Henry's best policy was to let sleeping kings lie?

The Grey Friars, taking their name from the colour of their garments, were Franciscans who came to England in 1224, around a year before the death of their founder, St Francis of Assisi. It is tradition that the friary in Leicester was founded by the 6th Earl of Leicester, Simon de Montfort, though this is unlikely.

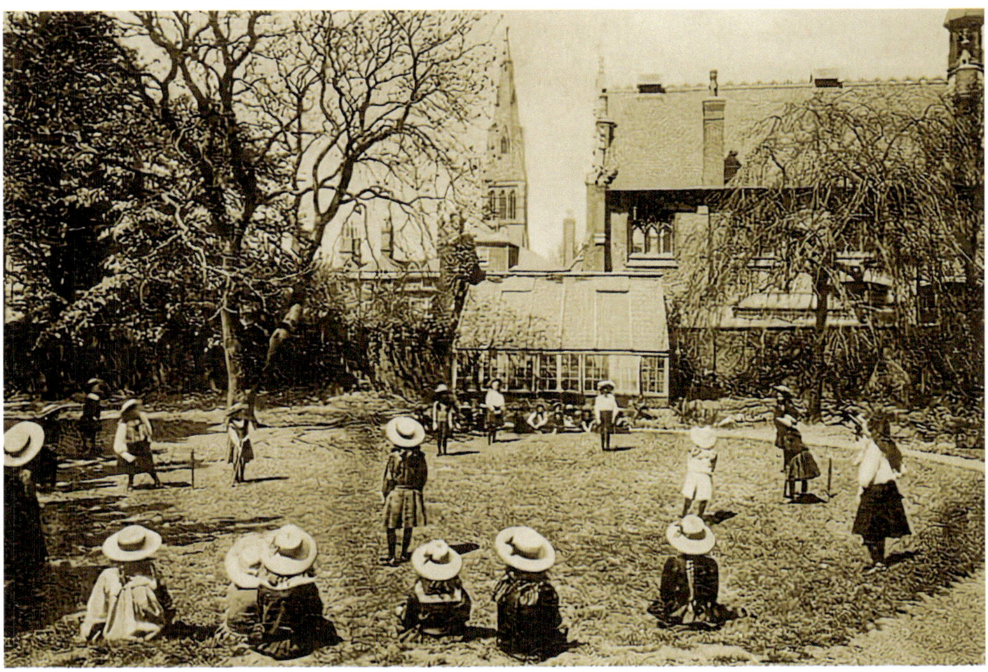

Wyggeston Girls' Junior School at 17 Friar Lane, located near to the site where the remains of Richard III were discovered.

The Grey Friars friary once occupied a large, walled precinct west of Leicester's Saturday marketplace. It was situated between two key medieval thoroughfares: Friar Lane and St Francis' Lane (now Peacock Lane). These streets connected the original high street (Highcross Street) and the south gate to the Saturday market, making the location ideal for friars to beg for alms.

On 10 November 1538, the friary was surrendered to King Henry VIII's commissioners. At that time, only seven friars remained, and the institution was impoverished, relying heavily on alms for survival.

By the late sixteenth century, Robert Herrick (1540–1618) – a wealthy alderman, former mayor and Member of Parliament for Leicester – had acquired the land. According to the Mayoral Roll:

'For some years prior to his death, he resided in a mansion house within the precincts and grounds of the dissolved Grey Friars monastery, nearly opposite St Martin's church.'

Herrick built his house in the southeastern part of the grounds, while the rest of the precinct was transformed into gardens and orchards. The property remained in the Herrick family until 1711, when Robert's great-grandson, Samuel Herrick, sold it.

In the following decades, the land was gradually divided and sold. In 1743, New Street was laid across the site, and by 1759, a fine townhouse had been built on part of the land which survives today as 17 Friar Lane. In 1776, Greyfriars House was sold to Thomas Pares, who later founded the bank Pares & Co. in 1800, located in the garden's northeast corner.

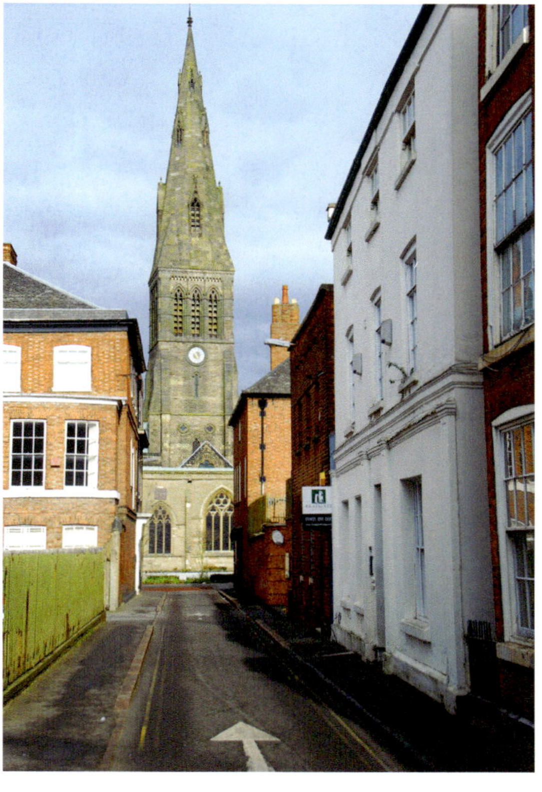

New Street, constructed across former Greyfriars land by Thomas Noble, who bought the estate in 1711.

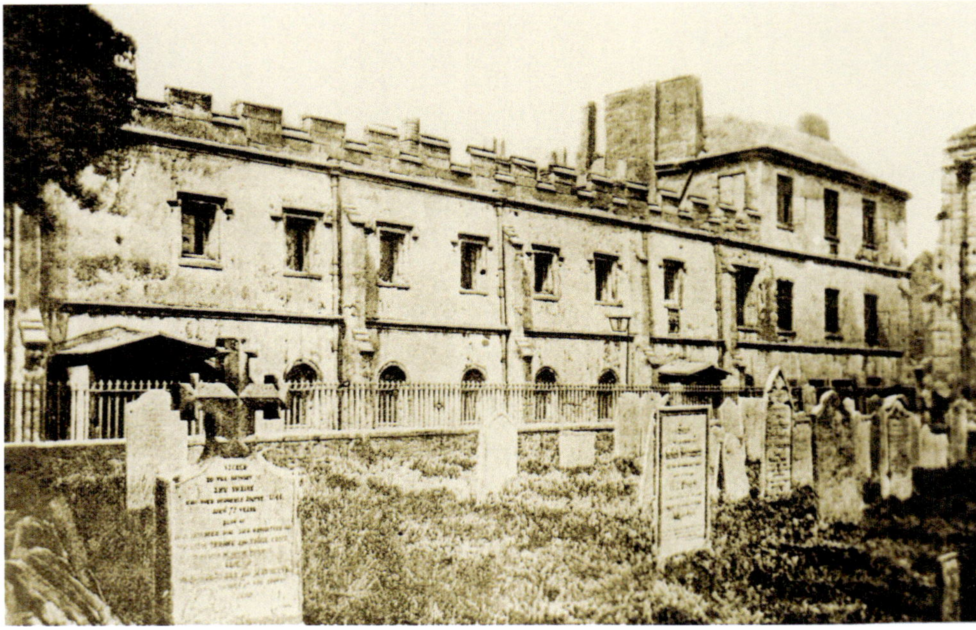

St Ursula's Hospital, demolished in 1876 when the Wyggeston Boys' School was built.

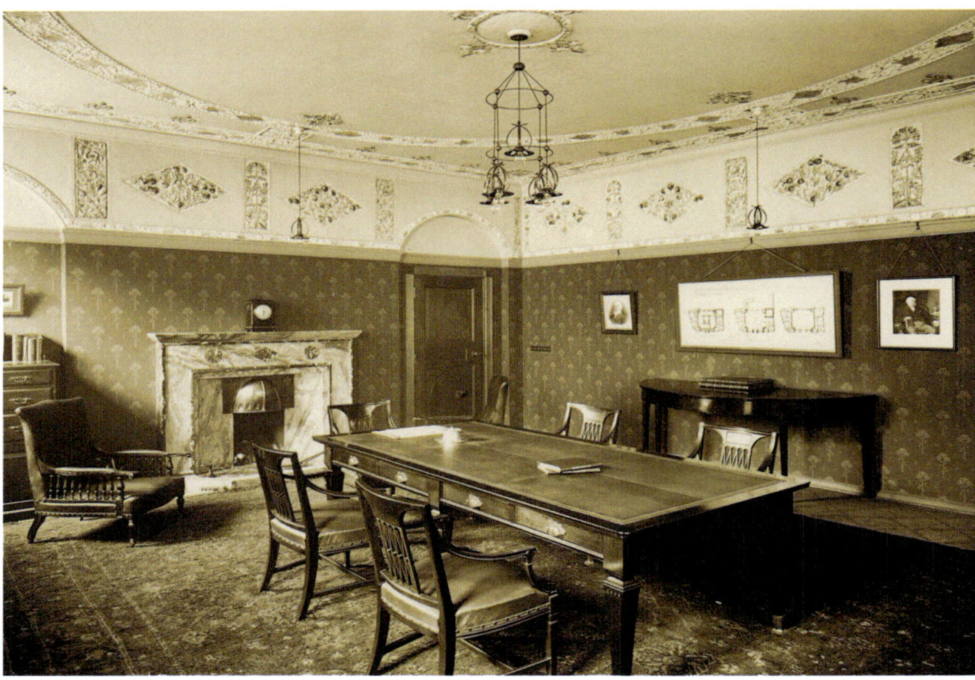

The office of the former Pares Bank, regarded as one of the most elegant banks in Leicester. It was designed by J. B. Everard & S. Perkins Pick in 1901.

Herrick's mansion was demolished in 1871 to make way for Greyfriars, which was laid out in 1873. The remaining land was then sold for commercial development. Part of the property at 17 Friar Lane was sold in 1863 to Alderman Newton's Boys' School and after 1915, Leicestershire County Council acquired the remaining land. Modern office buildings were erected in the 1920s and 1930s and used until 1965, when County Hall at Glenfield opened. These buildings were later occupied by Leicester City Council, and the remaining garden became a staff car park. By this time, all visible traces of the friary had vanished.

Leicester Abbey

The Abbey of Saint Mary de Pratis was an Augustinian religious house founded in 1143 by Robert de Beaumont, 2nd Earl of Leicester. It grew to become the wealthiest religious establishment in Leicestershire. Through patronage and donations the abbey gained the advowsons of countless churches throughout England, and acquired a considerable amount of land, and several manorial lordships.

Cardinal Wolsey died at the abbey on 29 November 1530 on his way from York to London, having been accused by Henry VIII of high treason. The Abbey was closed by Henry VIII in 1538 during the English Reformation. The buildings and land were handed to the landed gentry. William Parr, the brother of Catherine Parr, the sixth and last wife of Henry VIII, constructed a mansion on the site.

William Cavendish, the first Earl of Devonshire, acquired the property in 1613, and it became known as Cavendish House. The house was used by Charles I after the siege of Leicester in 1645. After he left, it is said that his soldiers gutted the building. A charred stone window frame is still visible today.

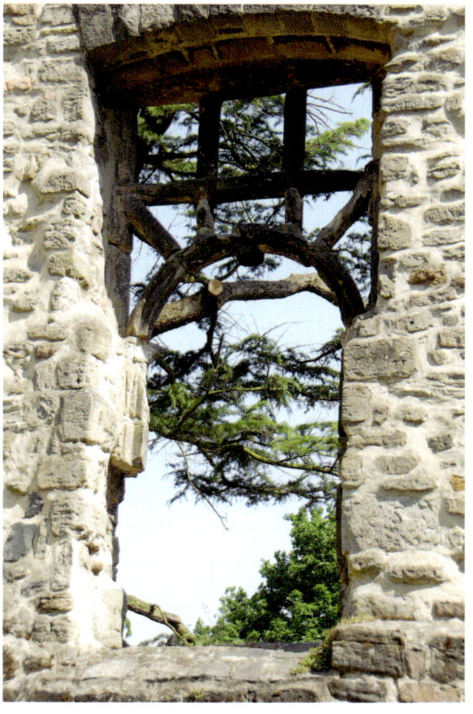

Cavendish House in Abbey Park, ruined in 1645 during the English Civil War.

In 1925, the Earl of Dysart gifted 32 acres of the Leicester Abbey grounds to the town of Leicester, the deed signed on 31 December of that year. Abbey Park officially opened in April 1932 as a public recreation area, featuring sports facilities and incorporating the ruins of Cavendish House along with the excavated remains of the Abbey. Later that year, the famous Leicester Pageant was staged in the park, the first of many public events.

The Newarke

The Church of the Annunciation of Our Lady of the Newarke was founded by Henry Plantagenet, 3rd Earl of Leicester, as a 'liberty', meaning it had its own jurisdiction and was independent of the laws and control of Leicester's main borough. This autonomy allowed it to develop its own institutions, including a collegiate church and a hospital. The Earl intended it to serve as a religious and charitable foundation, and over time it became a prestigious site, housing relics and royal burials.

The College and hospital were formally established by a Papal Bull issued by Pope John XXII on 13 June 1330, with the foundation document sealed in London on 20 January 1331.

Collegiate churches were run by a college of canons, a group of clergy who lived communally and maintained daily worship and religious services. These churches were 'extra-parochial', meaning they were not under diocesan control.

The hospital was designed to accommodate a warden and four chaplains (all priests living together, and instructed to avoid taverns and marketplaces), fifty poor and infirm people, including twenty permanent residents, and five women to care for them. Permanent residents were to be 'poor, blind, lame, maimed or suffering from an incurable disease'.

The church stood on the site now occupied by the Hawthorn Building of De Montfort University. Fragments of the original structure remain and are displayed in the De Montfort University Heritage Centre. These are historically significant because the body of Richard III, brought from the Battle of Bosworth, lay in this church before being interred at Greyfriars. Nearby stood the Newarke (or Trinity) Hospital, which tradition claims was connected to the church by a tunnel – though this has never been found. The hospital building now serves as the administrative centre of De Montfort University, following its relocation to modern facilities on Western Boulevard.

In March 2023, Trinity Hospital merged with the Hospital of William Wyggeston to form a new charity, Wyggestons and Trinity Almshouses, continuing the founders' original mission to serve the people of Leicestershire.

A substantial wall was constructed around the perimeter of the college with gateways. The Newarke Gateway, now commonly referred to as the Magazine Gateway, has survived. At the Reformation, the establishment was not immediately affected but was later dissolved under Edward VI in 1548. In more recent times, a variety of buildings have occupied the area including a 'mental' hospital for women, housing, and factories. Much of the area is now covered by buildings belonging to De Montfort University as the successor to Leicester Polytechnic and, originally, the Leicester Schools of Art and Design, and Technology.

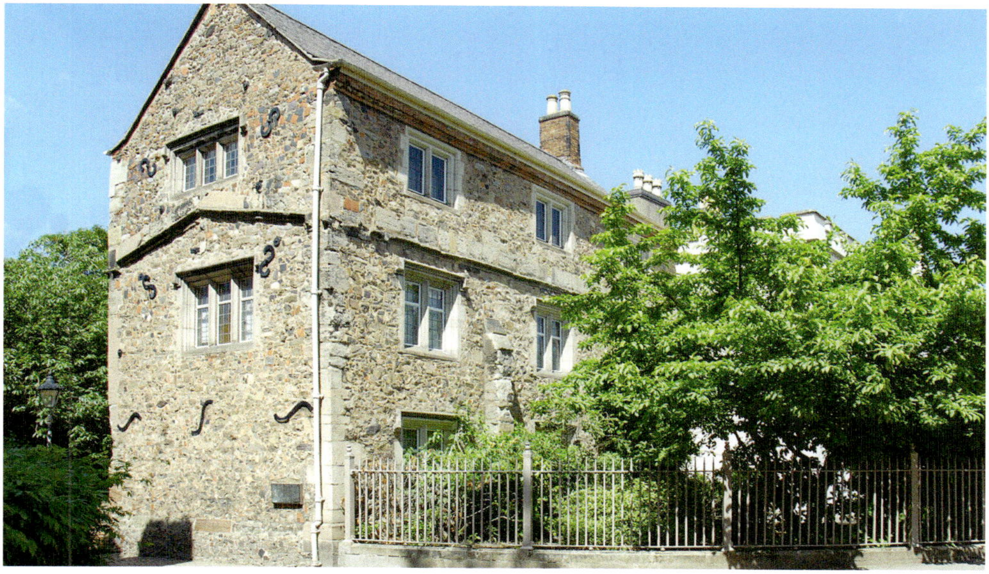

The Chantry House, constructed by William Wyggeston as a home for chantry priests employed to say Masses and prayers for his soul and for the royal family in the Church of the Annunciation of Our Lady of the Newarke.

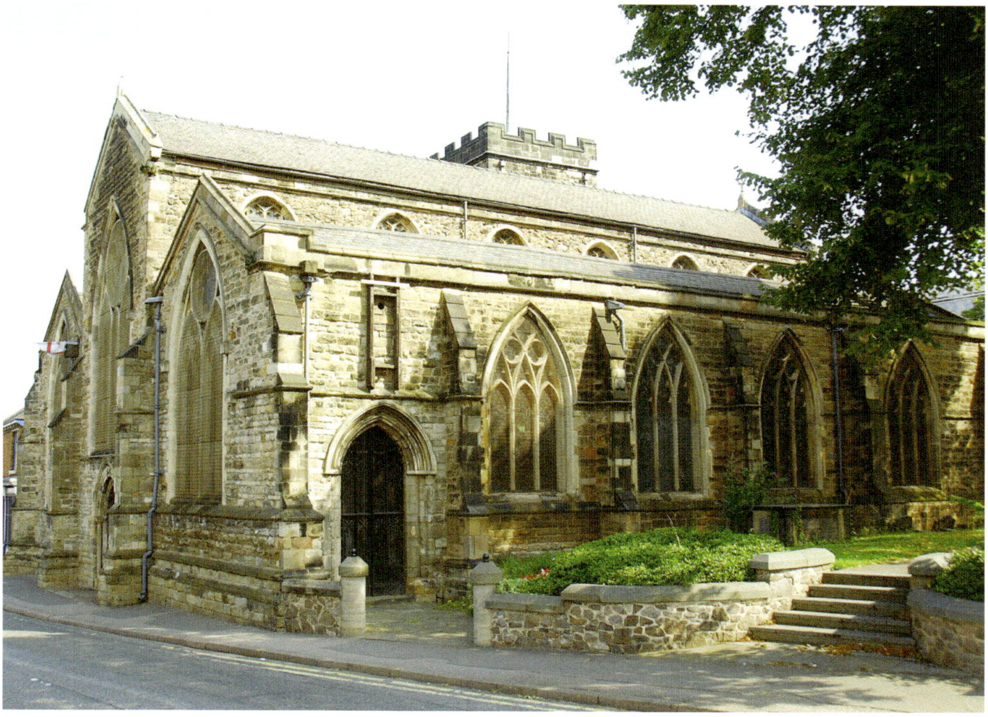

All Saints' Church is believed to be one of the six churches in Leicester listed in the Domesday Book.

The character of the Newarke area changed significantly in 1898 with the construction of a new bridge across the River Soar, linking the Newarke to the river's west bank. This new connection transformed what had been a quiet and historic part of the area into a busy through road. To accommodate the increased traffic, extensive demolitions were carried out to widen the old route, resulting in the loss of many homes. During this redevelopment, the open space in front of what is now the Hawthorn Building was created and later served as a Midland Red bus station. It has been redesigned on several recent occasions but is now an attractive quadrangle between several of the buildings in the university campus.

5

Markets and Merchants

Markets are organic and generic. In a sense, they last forever although they are ever-changing. They have a heritage that stretches back many centuries; but they are also transient and ephemeral. At close of day, they disappear.

Leicester was a town of many markets, and as with ecclesiastical establishments, modern placenames still guide us to where these ancient markets were held.

Wherever people lived, there were merchants who gathered in a conveniently open space to sell their goods. In Leicester, there were specific locations depending on the type of goods being sold. Possibly, the earliest marketplace in Leicester was on the site of, or close to, the Roman forum. Until the late seventeenth century, the town's meat market was held here, approximately where the Holiday Inn now stands in St Nicholas Circle. Again, possibly, nearby Holy Bones, by the side of St Nicholas Church, gained its name from the refuse accumulated over many centuries from the market.

Other guides to where markets once operated are stone crosses. This ancient meat market was bounded on one side by Red Cross Street, so named after the 'reed' cross that once stood on the site. Highcross Street is another example, marking the intersection of the two most important streets in the town, and where a market operated on Wednesdays

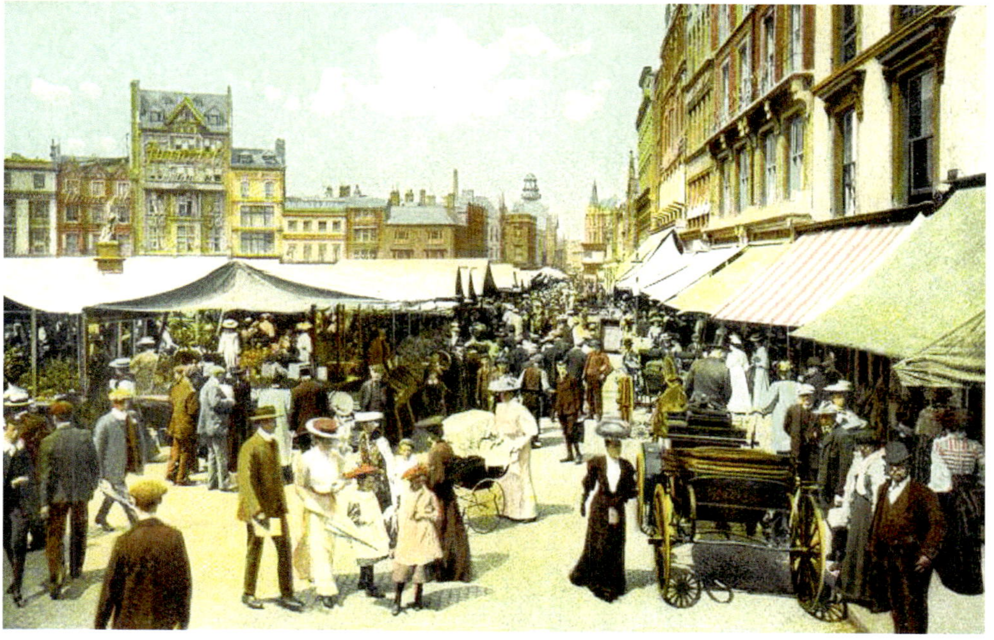

A colourful depiction of the Saturday Market in the late Victorian era.

selling dairy, produce, vegetables and fruit until 1884 when congestion prompted a move to the Saturday Market site – the present Leicester Market.

Today's marketplace has been a focus of social and cultural importance since the thirteenth century when it became the centre for trade in the area. The first recorded mention is in 1298 when 'a market took place bounded by the city walls and the corn wall'. The corn wall was used by horse dealers to display the speed of their animals like a racetrack. Possibly, this market is older. The Domesday Book uses the word 'Cheapside' which comes from the Danish word 'chepe', meaning sell.

Interestingly, royal charters apply to the land (the marketplace) and not to the market operating on that land. Royal charters protected the owner of the land on which a market or fair was held. The charter gave the landowner the power to prevent a rival market operating within a radius of 6.66 miles (approximately 10.7 km) which could attract traders away from an existing market and therefore reduce the landowner's income from rents. This unusually specific distance is said to relate to the ground that could be covered by a merchant to bring his stock to a market and return home afterwards, having stayed to trade for several hours.

Taking the markets as being evidence of the hub of a town's trading activity, it is fascinating to consider how and why that focus on Leicester shifted eastwards. The market at the high cross and those nearby were located on the main north-south route through the town, from Welford in the south through the south gate and on through the north gate and Woodgate (another ancient market site). Then, the trading emphasis moved to the present marketplace, and the approach from the south became London Road, Granby Street and Gallowtree Gate, thence to the clock tower and on through Churchgate to the north.

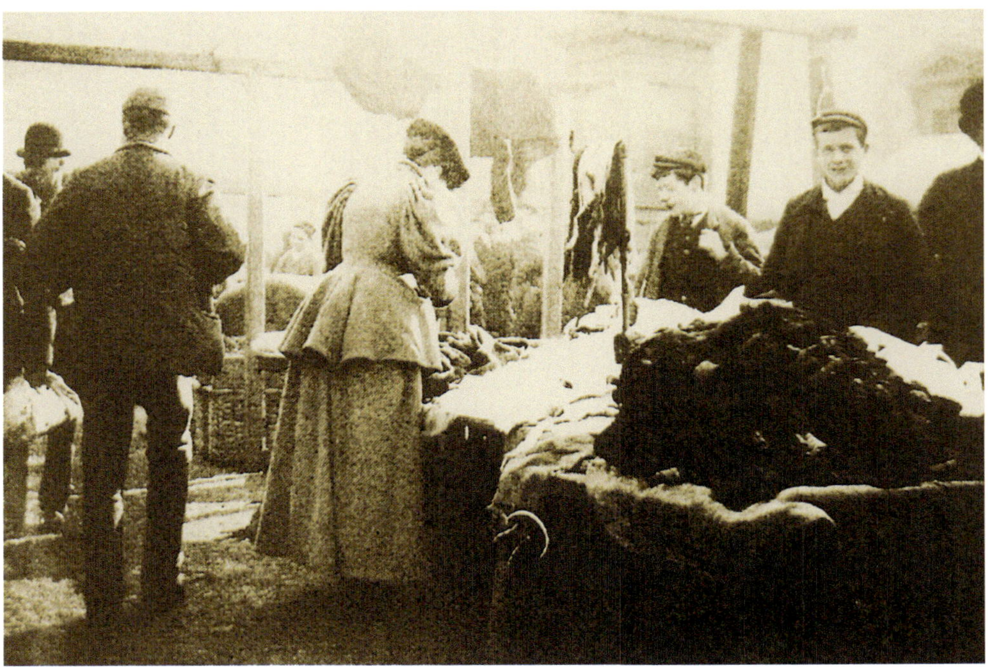

Buying clothes at Leicester Market. A photographic study by George Moore Henton (1861–1924).

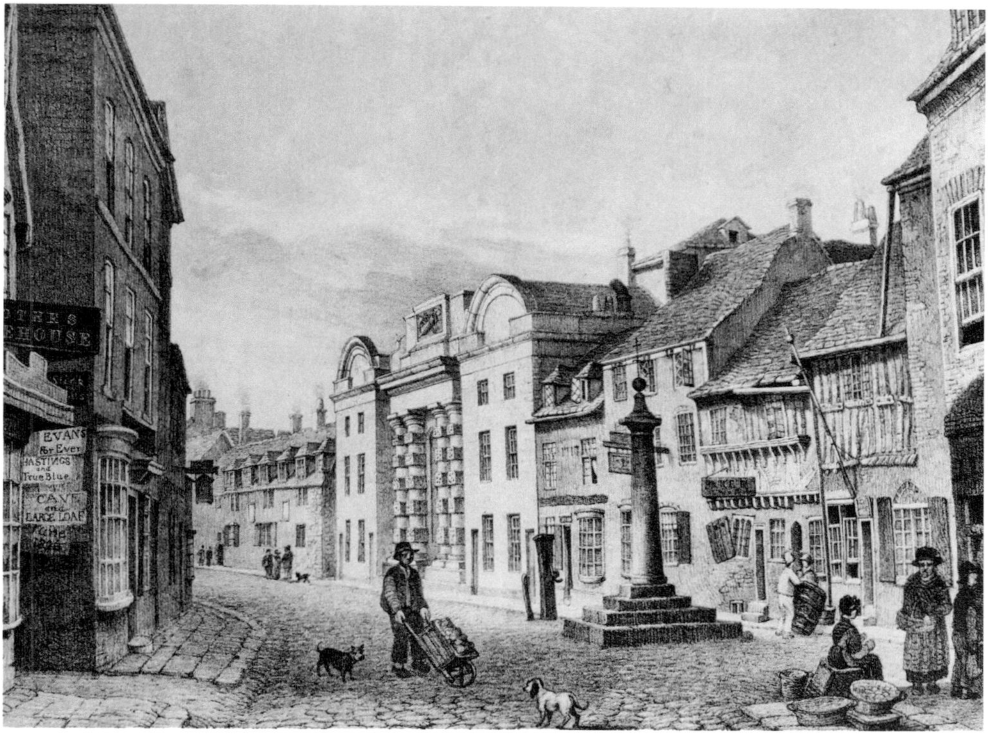

A detailed image of the High Cross by John Flower. Some of the buildings are still standing.

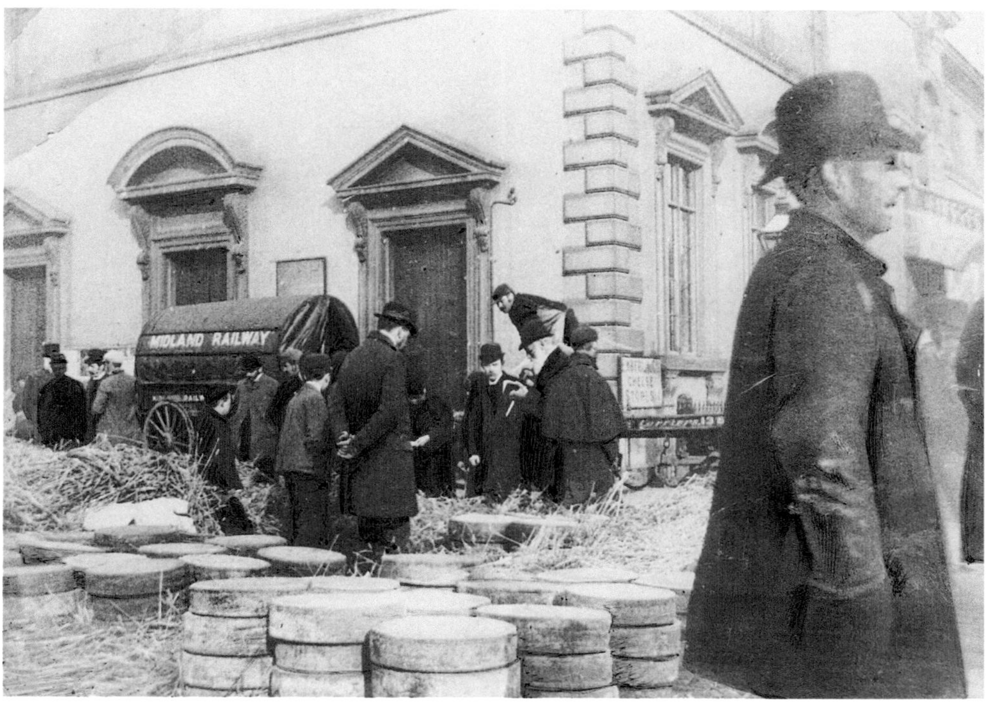

A cheese fair next to the Corn Exchange, photographed in around 1900.

The narrow alleys or *jitties* that now link the street to the marketplace were cut through for this reason.

Why the move to the Saturday Market area located in the extreme south-east corner of the old town? Certainly, it was spacious and was becoming a natural place for public events such as important proclamations and the sentencing of criminals. However, another reason could lie outside the town in the countryside of south Leicestershire. Here, the road from London through Market Harborough to Leicester was being improved by being turnpiked, making it a preferable route for merchants with heavily laden carts. Also, perhaps the size of the merchants' carts was increasing, making it difficult for them to access the town through the narrow south and north gates. In effect, Gallowtree Gate was a bypass, perhaps the first of many in Leicester.

Mention must also be made of the original cattle market, which was held where Town Hall Square now stands, and then moved, with the arrival of the Midland Railway, to land at Freemans Common on the old south field of the town from which a siding linked to the main railway line. Apparently, the move was a great relief to those who lived nearby and consequently suffered from the constant smell arising from the animals!

The Guild of Corpus Christi

The Guild of Corpus Christi was established in 1343 (some sources suggest 1350) as a religious and social fraternity composed of Leicester's wealthiest merchants and gentry. Its name, *Corpus Christi* – Latin for 'Body of Christ'– reflects its spiritual dedication to the Eucharist.

This influential guild played a central role in Leicester's medieval life. Members supported a chantry priest who offered prayers for their souls at the nearby Church of St Martin, now known as Leicester Cathedral.

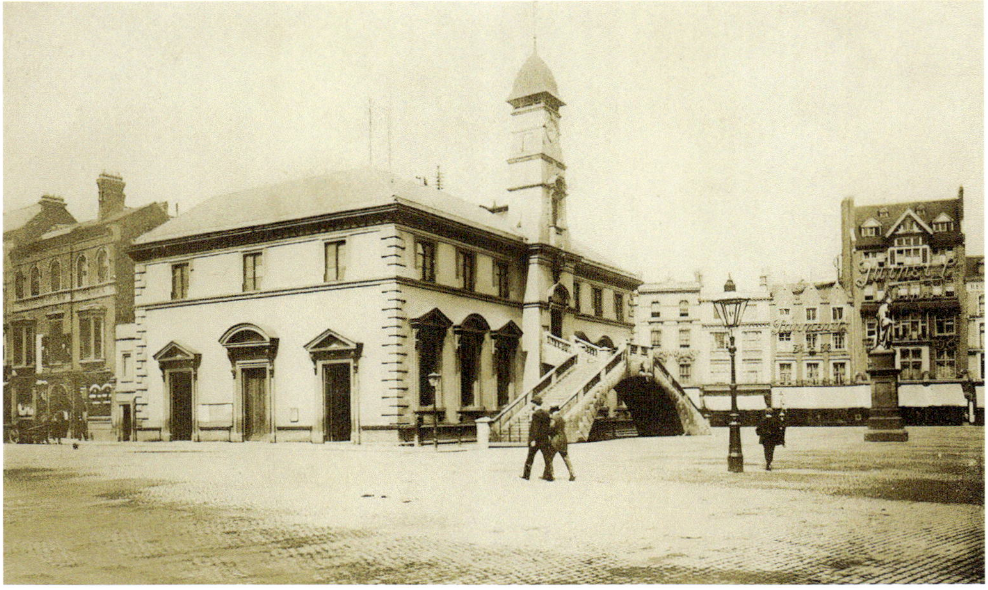

The Corn Exchange and marketplace in 1902.

To serve as its headquarters, the guild commissioned the construction of the Great Hall of the Leicester Guildhall around 1390. This hall became the venue for guild meetings, banquets, festivals, and ceremonial gatherings, especially during major religious celebrations. The Guildhall also included quarters for priests, which were later repurposed as part of Leicester's public library – one of the oldest in the country.

By the late fifteenth century, the Guildhall began to take on broader civic functions. In 1495, it became the meeting place for the Corporation of Leicester, and by 1563, it was officially recognised as Leicester's first Town Hall.

The Guild of Corpus Christi was eventually dissolved during the Reformation, along with other religious institutions, marking the end of its formal role in Leicester's governance and spiritual life. However, its legacy lives on in the Guildhall, which remains one of Leicester's most historic and cherished buildings.

The Merchant Guilds

The Merchant Guild of Leicester, known as the *Gilda Mercatoria*, holds a prominent place in the town's history, with its origins tracing back to the Norman period. Leicester's records provide valuable insight into the development and influence of guilds in medieval England.

The earliest surviving record of Leicester's Merchant Guild dates to 9 October 1196, though its formal establishment likely occurred earlier. In 1107, the first Norman Earl of Leicester granted the townspeople the right to form a 'Guild Merchant'. This guild was created for mutual protection and to regulate matters essential to the good governance of the town.

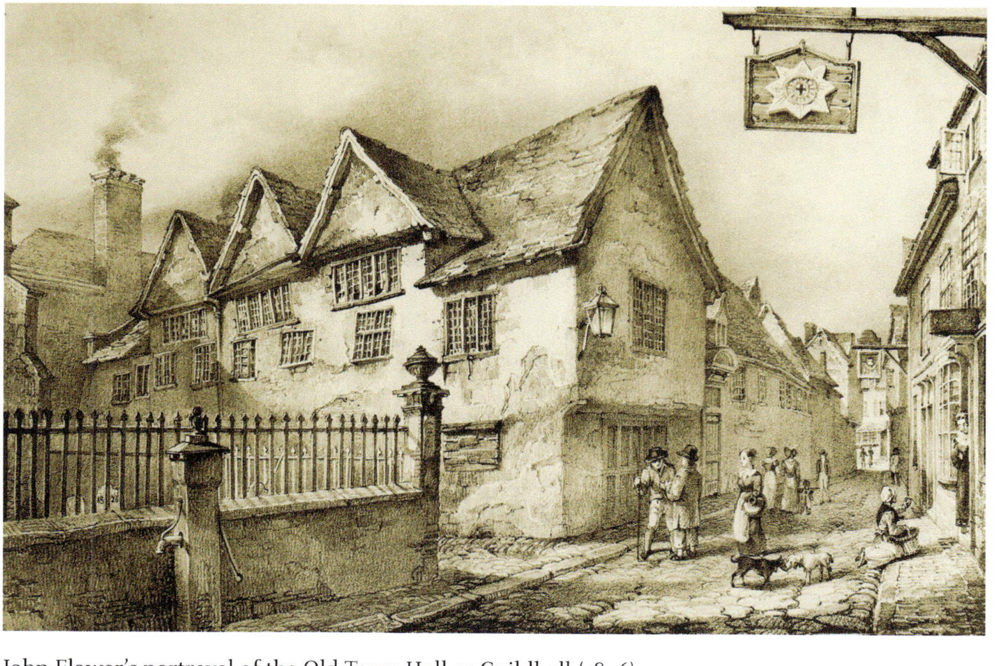

John Flower's portrayal of the Old Town Hall or Guildhall (1826).

Guilds in Leicester were not solely commercial entities. They often overlapped with religious and social functions, incorporating members from various walks of life. Leicester's guilds maintained common funds to support members in times of distress, enforced discipline through fines and fostered a strong sense of community and mutual aid.

The sixteenth century brought rapid and transformative changes. Leicester Abbey was dissolved in 1537, followed by the suppression of the College of St Mary in the Newarke and the town's various religious fraternities in 1545. By 1547, parish churches were stripped of their traditional adornments, and in 1548, Leicester's religious guilds were formally dissolved. Among these were the Guilds of St Margaret, St Mary and St Katherine, St George, Trinity, St John the Baptist, the Assumption and the Corpus Christi Guild, the most affluent of them all, which had gradually absorbed the original Merchant Guild.

Following the dissolution of these institutions, Leicester's municipal authorities took steps to maintain religious observance. In 1558, the Common Hall decreed that at least one person from every household must attend services held on Wednesdays and Fridays, in addition to Sunday worship, under penalty of a fine.

While the markets and merchant guilds were originally governed by the crown through the authority of the Norman overlords and their successors, power and authority gradually shifted over the centuries. The church and religious institutions gained increasing influence until the Reformation, and the merchant guilds eventually laid the foundation for local governance.

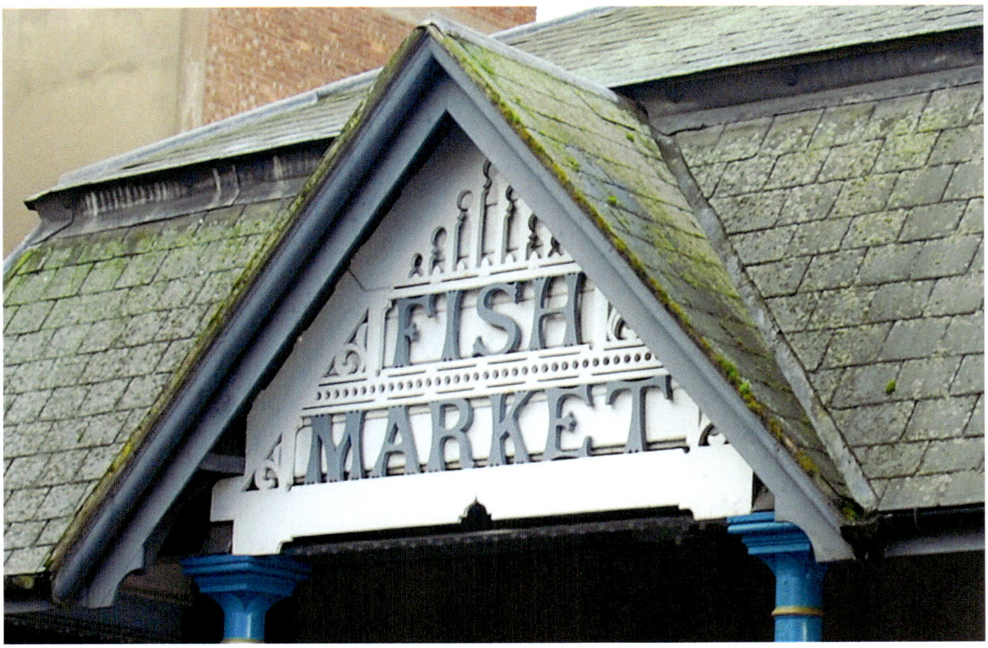

The entrance to the Victorian Fish Market which opened in autumn 1877.

The successors to these powers that existed in medieval Leicester still have an influence over us today, but in very different forms. The merchants are still with us, online as well as in the High Street, and one of Leicester's predominant business activities is in conveying goods from manufacturers to retailers and thence to consumers.

The church still has a strong influence, although attendance at formal services has lessened considerably. For many people, places of worship such as Leicester Cathedral, St Mary de Castro, St Margaret's and others, are more than buildings of heritage; they have a meaning that is much deeper and significant.

Local government, as in Leicester City Council, can trace its roots back to those early times, and despite the views of some residents, we live in a more democratic society than ever before, thanks in no small part to the radical social and political pioneers of the nineteenth century; but before that age, Leicester was to suffer, once again, the brutal effects of conflict.

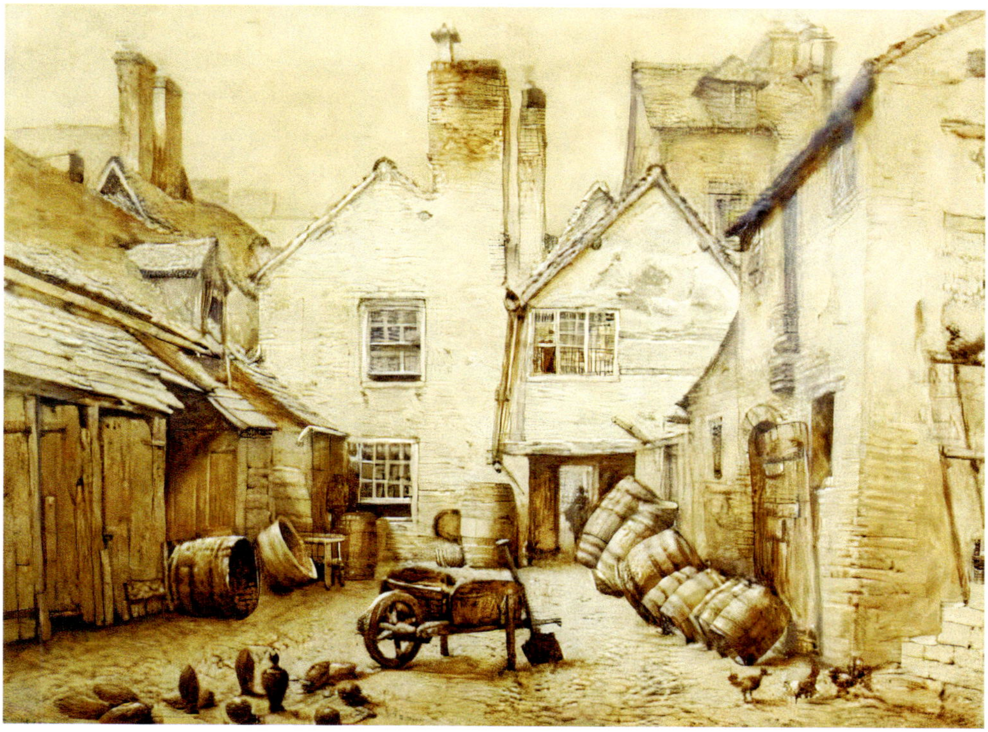

The yard of the Green Dragon pub in the late nineteenth century. The name has been retained in the modern Green Dragon Square.

6

Tolerance and Radicalism

Leicester has a history of religious tolerance. It also has a history of political radicalism. Sometimes, these two social groupings met, joined forces or chose to part company. But the Civil War period demonstrated that tolerance could fall by the wayside when other forces took control.

The Siege of Leicester

During the English Civil Wars, Leicester experienced one of the most brutal and consequential episodes of the conflict – the Siege of Leicester in May 1645. Leicester was a Parliamentarian stronghold, and its refusal to support King Charles I early in the war made it a target. The town had previously denied Charles entry in 1642, forcing him to stay outside its walls. This act of defiance likely contributed to the severity of the Royalist assault three years later.

Royalist forces, led by Prince Rupert, arrived with around 10,000 troops. Leicester's defenders numbered only around 2,000, including local volunteers. The town's medieval defences were in a sorry state, and were hastily reinforced by townspeople, including women and children, during the siege. On 30 May, Prince Rupert demanded surrender. When it was refused, a midnight assault began. The Royalists eventually broke through after fierce street-to-street fighting, with defenders making a final stand at the High Cross. Once inside the town, the Royalist troops unleashed a rampage.

As always in times of war, the residents, some of whom were probably unaware of the strategic issues, suffered greatly, losing loved ones and homes, and bore great deprivation. Over 700 civilians were killed, around 20 per cent of the town's population. Women were raped, homes looted and churches desecrated. Churches including St Martin's, St Margaret's and St Mary de Castro were directly involved in the fighting, used as defensive positions or burial sites

The sack of Leicester became a symbol of Royalist cruelty and was used as evidence in Charles I's trial for treason in 1649.

A retired clergyman once told me that in his time as a minister serving in Leicestershire parishes he could sense an inherited 'mood' within his congregations that reflected the stance taken by each community during the English Civil Wars. He spoke of a certain 'dourness' in the villages that had supported the Parliamentarians, and even suggested that the ancient Fosse Way – now the A46 – was a physical divide between the communities that supported the King and those that supported the Parliamentarians.

The hurt of the civil war period ran deep. So deep that it permeated down through subsequent generations. No war can be described as 'civil', and the English 'civil' wars split families as well as communities. The darker side of humanity came to the fore. In Kibworth, after the Restoration, the intruding minister and his pregnant wife were chased out of the parish by armed men.

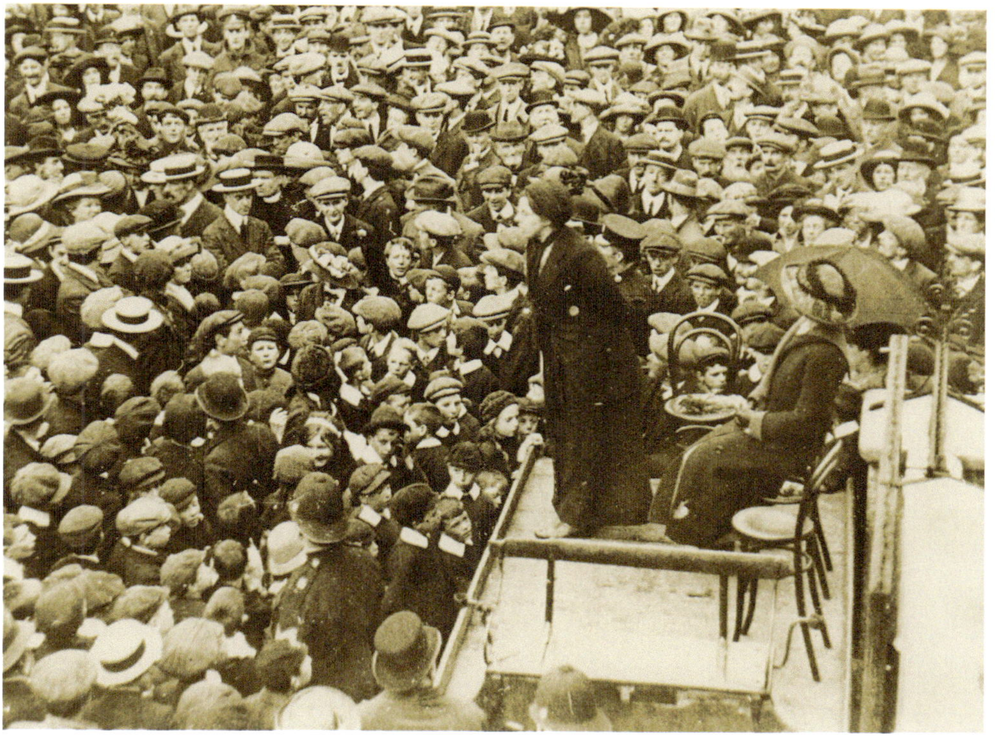

A suffragette rally in the Market Place.

A Certain Tolerance

Then came a time when, to quote the title of a book by the late Christopher Hill, the 'world turned upside down'. He drew the title, significantly, from that of a ballad published on a broadside in the middle of the 1640s as a protest against the policies of Parliament relating to the celebration of Christmas. Following the Toleration Act of 1689, across the country – including Leicester – a level of freedom of religious expression was given to 'protestant dissenters'. Under this umbrella term a variety of religious and quasi-political groups emerged after years of conflict and suppression.

The Great Meeting

The Great Meeting, home of the Leicester Unitarians, was built in 1708 and is thought to be the oldest complete brick building in the city, as well as one of the most important historic buildings in Leicester still serving the purpose for which it was constructed.

The history of the building and those who have worshipped within it dates back even further to the early followers of the Presbyterian sect who in 1680 were given a licence to meet in a barn near to the present site of the Leicester Royal Infirmary. Presbyterians were those who disliked the formalities and traditions of the Anglican Church but who believed that it was better to stay and try to change attitudes from within rather than to break away.

Two years later, the early Congregationalists were known to be meeting in another barn near Millstone Lane. It is possible that this building was a remnant of the Greyfriars complex, and it is recorded that the early Methodists in Leicester also gathered here. They came to share the same minister, and in a short time became united in their beliefs. As the congregation grew, a permanent church was needed, and the Great Meeting was planned, and opened in 1708. The form of worship in the church became Unitarian at the beginning of the nineteenth century, and its members were a very strong influence on the political and civic life for many more years, even to the present day.

In essence, Unitarianism is a Christian denomination which takes an open-minded and individualistic approach to religion and so allows for a very wide range of beliefs and interpretations. The freedom of Unitarians to search for meaning in life in a responsible way and to reach their own conclusions is counter to many nonconformist denominations which believe in some degree of exclusivity. As its name implies, it believes in the concept

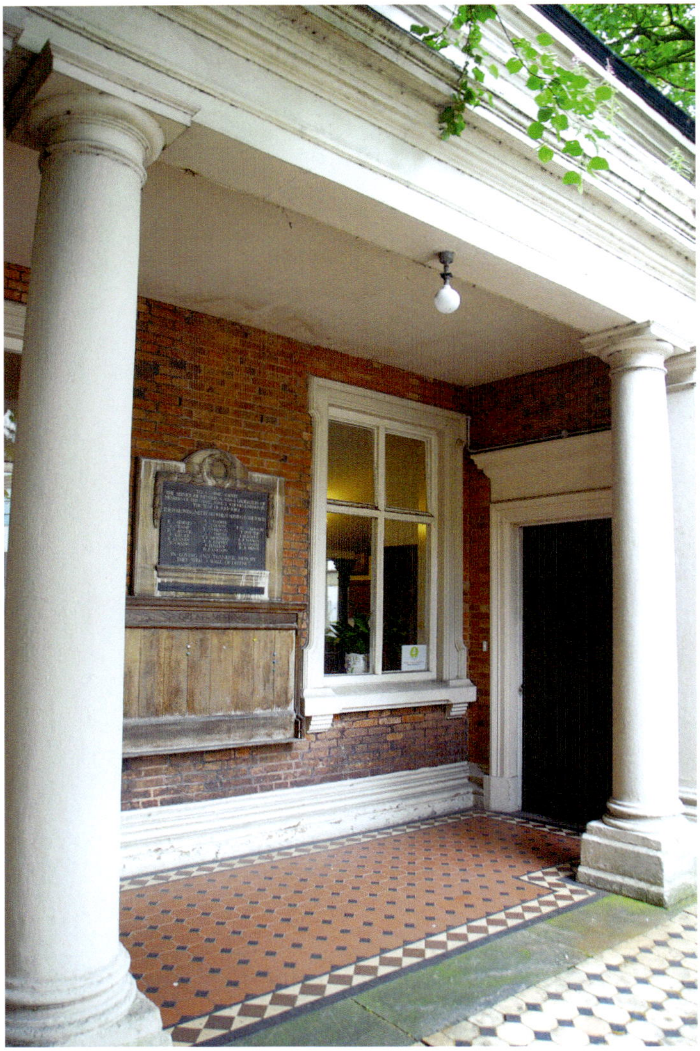

The 'Great Meeting', attended by many of Leicester's most influential political leaders. The first seven mayors of the town following municipal reform in 1835 were Unitarians.

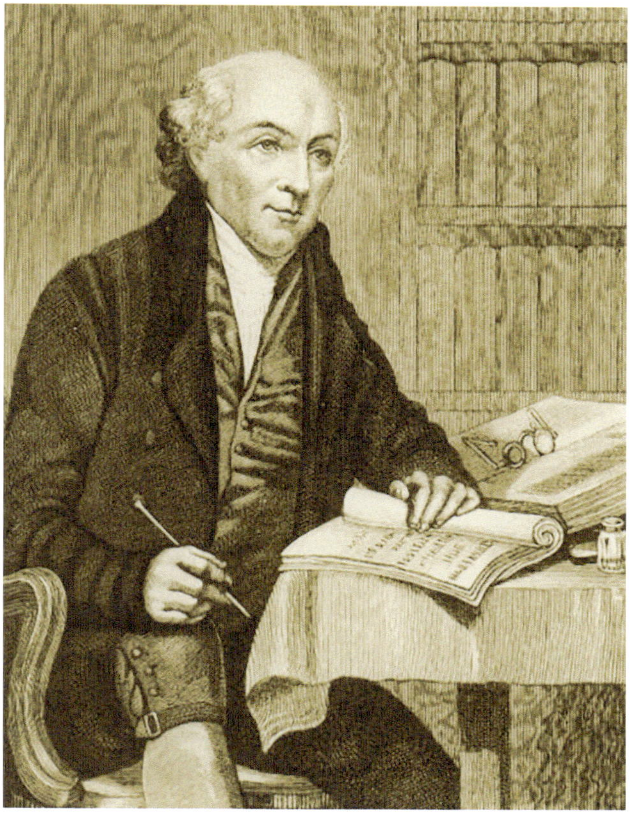

William Carey, the pioneering Baptist minister and missionary who lived in Leicester from 1789 to 1793 and served as pastor of the Harvey Lane Baptist Church.

of one God but not that of the Trinity (as in God the Father, God the Son and God the Holy Spirit). Unitarians want religion to be broad, inclusive and tolerant. Unitarianism can therefore include people who are Christian, Jewish, Buddhist, Pagan and Atheist. Today there are around 7,000 Unitarians in the United Kingdom, served by around 150 ministers. The Great Meeting here in Leicester is still very much part of the city and merges successfully into the surrounding businesses, welcoming shoppers and workers without qualification.

In 1835, the Municipal Reform Act paved the way for a dramatic change in how Leicester was governed. The 'old guard' of the previous Corporation was rejected, making way for a group of enlightened and responsible leaders, many of whom came from the ranks of the Unitarians, and were industrialists, businessmen, entrepreneurs and benefactors.

William Carey and the Harvey Lane Chapel

The founder of the Baptist Missionary Society, William Carey, moved to Leicester in 1789 from his native Northamptonshire, to become the minister of the Harvey Lane Chapel. The church was located on the corner of Harvey Lane and Thornton Lane, and for the four years he remained in the town, he lived in a small cottage opposite the church, supplementing his income by shoemaking and running a small school.

The Harvey Lane Chapel was destroyed in a fire in 1921. It was rebuilt as a Memorial Hall but demolished in 1963. His cottage was removed at the same time to make way for the Southgates Underpass and Holiday Inn development. The various relics that had previously made up a small museum in Carey's Cottage are now at the Central Baptist Church in Charles Street. The elevated footpath between the Holiday Inn and the St Nicholas Circle multi-storey car park is named Harvey Walk and follows the approximate line of the former Harvey Lane. There is a commemorative plaque referring to the site of Carey's Cottage near the Holiday Inn's reception.

Carey was mainly self-taught, but became fluent in Greek, Latin and Hebrew as well as knowledgeable in science and history. While in Leicester he wrote his *The Enquirer*, which is still regarded as the finest missionary treatise ever written. The Baptist Missionary Society was founded in 1792, largely because of Carey's influence, and in 1793 he travelled with his family to India. He worked as a foreman in an indigo factory in Calcutta until setting up a church there before moving on to Serampore in 1799.

He was made Professor of Sanskrit and Bengali at Fort William Cottage in Calcutta in 1801 and in 1805 opened a mission chapel there. He was a prodigious translator, responsible with others of translating the Bible into six Indian languages, and the New Testament into twenty-three more. He died at Serampore in 1834.

From the seventeenth to the nineteenth centuries, the General and Particular Baptists formed the largest body of dissenters in Leicester, playing a significant role in the city's religious life. One of the earliest Baptist congregations, the General Baptists of Friar Lane Chapel, dates to 1651, marking a long-standing presence in the area. In 1672, John Bunyan, the author of *The Pilgrim's Progress*, preached in Leicester, likely addressing both Baptist and Congregationalist audiences. The city also became home to Robert Hall (1764–1831), a renowned Baptist preacher known for his eloquence and influence. Later, the establishment of Victoria Road Baptist Church further reflected the continued growth and vitality of the Baptist movement in Leicester.

Radical Leicester

Dissenters and radical thinkers prosper in a tolerant society. Leicester in the eighteenth and nineteenth centuries was a hotbed of radical political and social movements driven by industrial change, religious dissent and demands for democratic reform. These thinkers, leaders and the organisations they created or supported varied widely in their beliefs and aims.

Jonathan Rembrandt Hall Bairstow was a prominent Chartist leader and orator who settled in Leicester in the early 1840s. Originally from Yorkshire, Bairstow was known for his powerful speeches and sermons that blended religious rhetoric with Chartist principles. He edited *The Chartist Pilot*, a Leicester-based newspaper, and was involved in several arrests and trials due to his activism. Despite early popularity, his reputation suffered due to personal misconduct and financial mismanagement, leading to a split among Leicester Chartists.

Thomas Pendrill Bailey was a leading figure in Leicester's trade union movement during the 1860s and 1870s. He helped establish the Leicester & Leicestershire Framework Knitters Union, which laid the foundation for the Trades Council in 1872. Bailey was also active in the Leicester Democratic Association and ran as a 'working man' candidate for the school board, topping the poll in 1871. He advocated for arbitration over strikes and was instrumental in campaigns against exploitative practices in the hosiery industry.

William Baines, a draper and member of Bond Street Chapel, was a nonconformist activist who opposed the compulsory payment of church rates. In 1840, he was imprisoned for refusing to pay these rates, sparking widespread protest and national support. His case highlighted the tension between the Church of England and dissenting religious groups. Baines was later elected to the Town Council while still in prison and remained active in the Liberation Society, which campaigned for religious freedom.

Thomas Cooper, another influential Chartist, was known for his poetic and religiously infused speeches in Leicester's Market Place. He collaborated with Bairstow but later distanced himself due to Bairstow's misconduct. Cooper's faction, the Shakespearian Chartists, emphasized moral and educational uplift alongside political reform.

Following the Reform Act of 1832, Leicester's politics were dominated by Reformers, particularly wealthy nonconformist businessmen. They challenged the old corporation and pushed for municipal reform. However, internal divisions and disillusionment with national Whig policies led to setbacks. The campaign against church rates, supported by figures like Baines, was a major local issue that reflected broader national tensions between church and dissent.

Thomas Cook (1808–92) revolutionised travel by making it accessible to the masses. Born in Derbyshire and raised in modest circumstances, he began his career as a cabinet

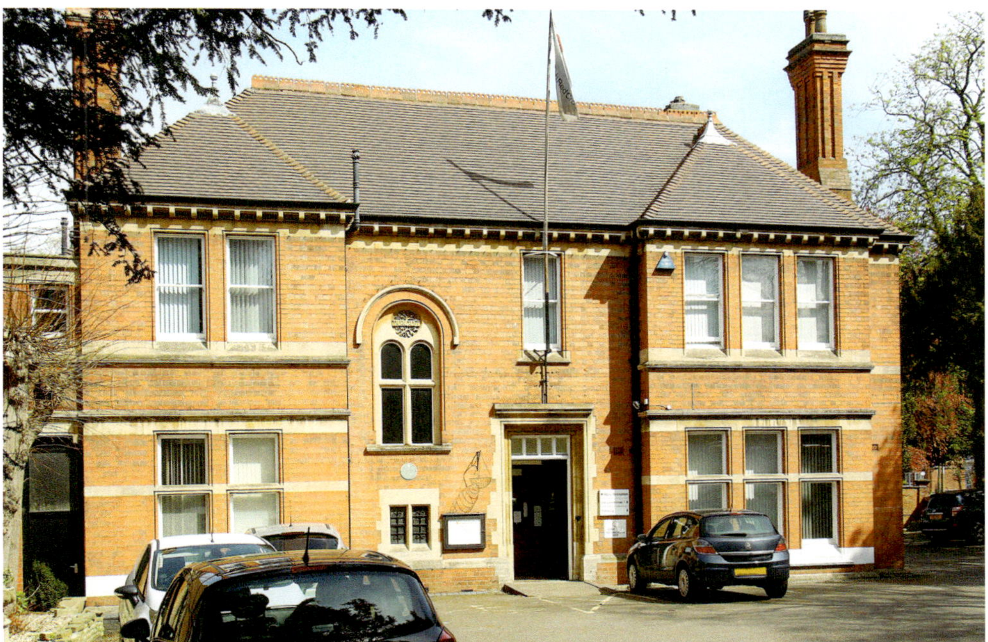

'Thorncroft' in London Road, the retirement home of travel entrepreneur, temperance leader and Baptist preacher Thomas Cook.

maker and Baptist preacher. A passionate supporter of the temperance movement, Cook believed that organised travel could offer a wholesome alternative to alcohol and vice. In 1841, he arranged his first group excursion, a railway journey from Leicester to Loughborough for a temperance meeting.

Cook expanded his services to include leisure travel across the UK and Europe, eventually founding Thomas Cook & Son with his son, John Mason Cook. The company introduced innovations such as hotel coupons, traveller's cheques and guided tours, making travel more convenient and affordable. Cook's efforts culminated in a global tour in 1874, and by the time of his retirement in 1878, he had laid the foundations of the modern travel industry.

Cook also responded to the poverty he saw in Leicester. From his offices in Granby Street, he would prepare portions of food, delivered by his staff to those in most need. To some extent, he was also aware of the benefits that the Industrial Revolution could bring. His offices were the first buildings in Leicester to be connected to a water supply piped from Thornton Reservoir.

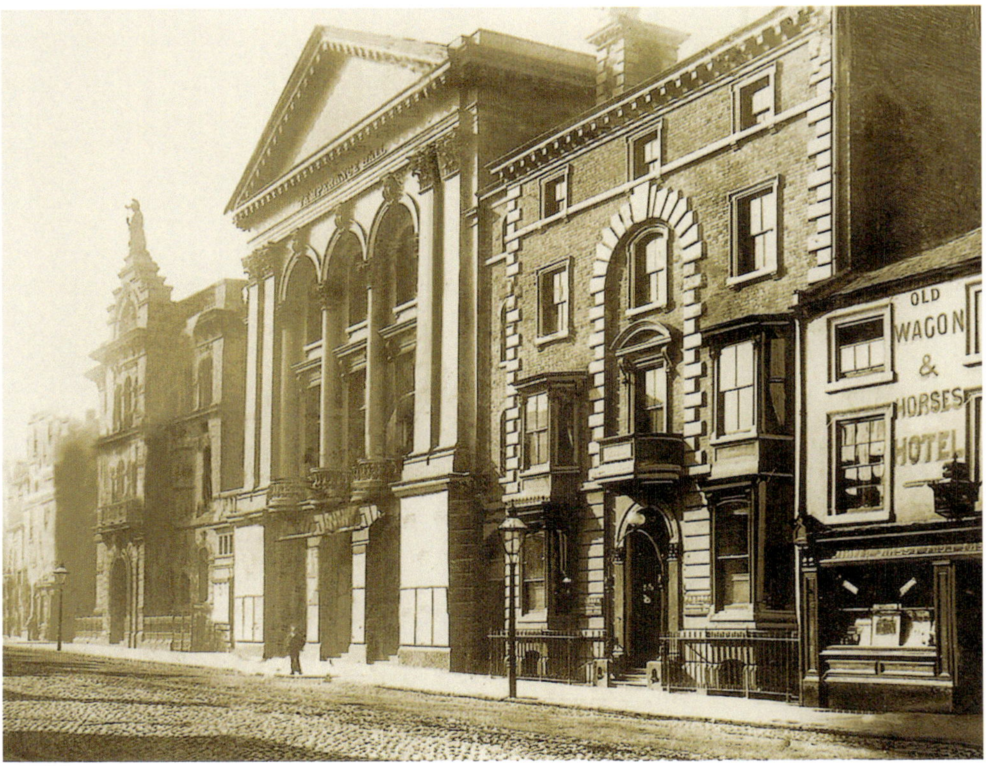

Thomas Cook's temperance hall and offices in Granby Street.

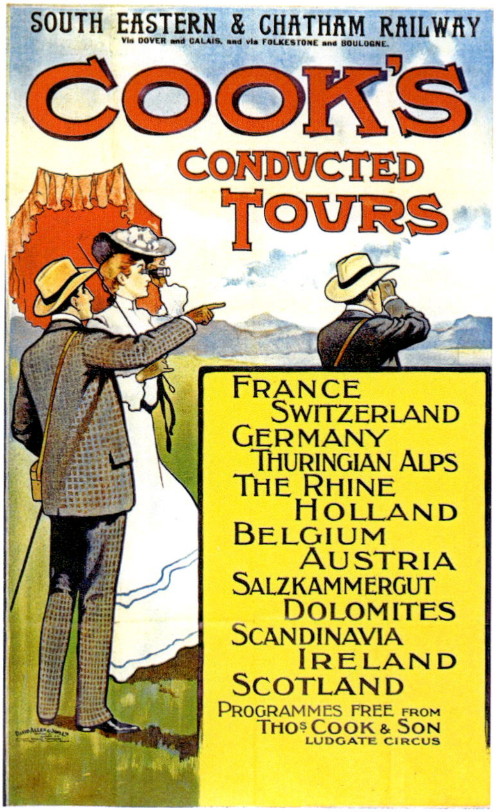

A poster for one of Thomas Cook's famous and popular 'Cooks tours', bringing the opportunity of worldwide travel to the working classes.

The Leicester March of the Unemployed

The 1912 Leicester March of the Unemployed was a powerful demonstration of working-class frustration during a period of economic hardship and industrial change. As unemployment rose due to mechanisation and job cuts in key industries like footwear and hosiery, hundreds of jobless workers took to the streets to demand action. The march was part of a broader wave of protests across Britain, but in Leicester, it was marked by a strong sense of local solidarity and urgency. Protesters gathered at the Corn Exchange, a traditional rallying point, and marched through the city, voicing their grievances about poverty, lack of work and inadequate support from local authorities.

Though not as nationally prominent as the 1905 march to London, the 1912 protest reflected deep-rooted tensions in Leicester's industrial economy. It was driven by grassroots organisation and supported by trade unionists and social reformers. The march helped galvanise public awareness and contributed to growing pressure on municipal leaders to address unemployment and improve welfare provisions. It stands as a testament to Leicester's long tradition of civic activism and working-class resistance.

The three key leaders of the 1912 Leicester March of the Unemployed were Amos Sherriff (1856–1945), Frederick Lewis Donaldson (1860–1953) and George 'Sticky' White.

Born in one of Leicester's poorest districts, Amos Sherriff began working at the age of six in the Spinney Hill Brick Works and remained illiterate until his twenties. He found purpose through the Salvation Army, where he learned to read and write and became a

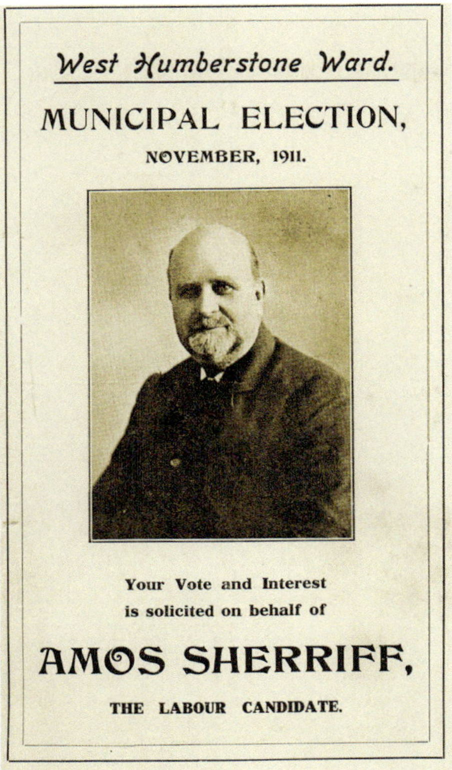

An election poster for Amos Sherriff who co-led the Leicester March of the Unemployed in 1912. He became Leicester's first Labour Lord Mayor.

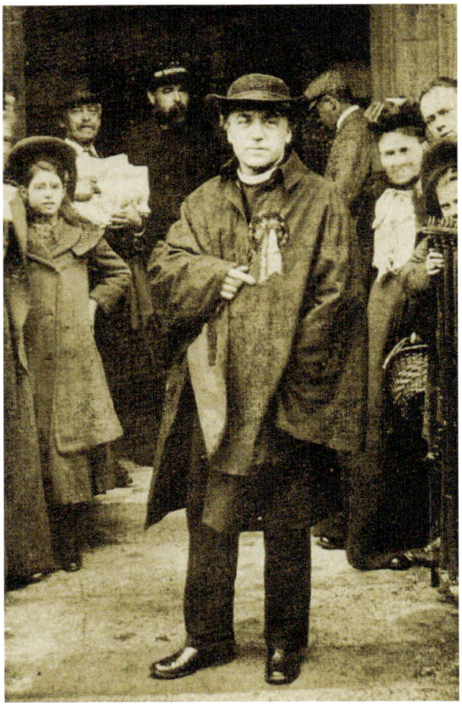

Revd Frederick Donaldson, 'chaplain to Leicester's unemployed', during the 1912 march. The following year he led a deputation of clergy to the Prime Minister demanding women's suffrage.

street preacher. His deep empathy for the working class led him into politics, where he became a powerful advocate for the unemployed. Sherriff was a key organiser of both the 1905 and 1912 marches of the unemployed, and in 1922, he became Leicester's first Labour Lord Mayor.

A Church of England priest and committed Christian Socialist, Frederick Donaldson served for twenty-two years as vicar of St Mark's Church, Leicester, where he ministered to some of the city's poorest communities. He was a passionate advocate for social justice and peace, opposing the First World War and supporting women's suffrage. At St Mark's, he commissioned a series of dramatic murals as an altar backdrop depicting the poverty, pain and sorrow experienced by the working-class parishioners he served.

These murals were designed to reflect the harsh realities of life in Leicester's industrial districts, where issues like infant mortality, child labour, underpayment and premature death were common. Donaldson believed that the church should not only offer spiritual guidance but also stand as a voice for justice and compassion. The murals served as a visual sermon, reinforcing his message of social reform and Christian duty.

Although the church closed in 1986 and was later restored as the Empire Conference and Banqueting Centre, the murals are preserved behind protective internal walls as part of Leicester's radical and artistic heritage.

Donaldson co-led the 1912 march, using his position to draw national attention to the plight of the unemployed. He later became a Canon of Westminster Abbey, where he famously preached the sermon that inspired Gandhi's publication of the 'Seven Social Sins'.

George White, known affectionately as 'Sticky' due to his habit of walking everywhere with a stick, was a trade union leader and secretary of Leicester's Unemployed Committee. Though initially hesitant about protest marches, he joined Sherriff and Donaldson in leading the 1912 demonstration. White represented the growing influence of organised labour in Leicester's civic life and played a crucial role in uniting workers behind the cause of unemployment relief. However, and sadly, despite his work in improving the lives of many Leicester people, he committed suicide.

Working-class Agitation

Leicester was a focal point for working-class agitation in the early 1800s, with movements such as Luddism and Chartism sparking widespread demonstrations and riots. In 1819, thousands of framework knitters protested wage cuts, joined by women and children carrying placards that read 'We perish with Hunger'. Riots erupted in places like Wigston Magna in 1825, and in 1833, female workers at a worsted-spinning factory were sentenced for assault and riotous assembly. The Chartist riot of 1842 saw 12,000 people clash with police and Yeomanry, resulting in significant damage and arrests. In 1848, the Workhouse Riots highlighted the desperation of the unemployed, with women actively participating by collecting stones to use against the authorities.

The Leicester Suffragettes

The suffragette movement in Leicester was marked by passionate activism, bold protest and a strong sense of community, with Alice Hawkins emerging as its most iconic figure.

A working-class shoe machinist, Hawkins became deeply involved in the campaign for women's voting rights, joining the Women's Social and Political Union (WSPU) in 1907. Her activism was militant and courageous – she was imprisoned five times for actions such as chaining herself to railings, throwing stones through government windows and disrupting political meetings, including one led by Winston Churchill.

Leicester's suffragette movement gained momentum with the establishment of a local WSPU branch and the opening of a dedicated shop on Bowling Green Street in 1910. This shop sold 'Votes for Women' merchandise and served as a hub for organizing protests and meetings. It also became a site of civil disobedience during the 1911 census, when women refused to be counted as a form of protest against their disenfranchisement.

Beyond Hawkins, other Leicester suffragettes like Lilian Lenton and Nellie Taylor also made headlines. Lenton was known for her daring escapes and militant actions, including arson, while Taylor, a mother of three, nearly died on hunger strike.

Leicester's industrial roots and tradition of radical politics made it fertile ground for the suffrage movement. Public speeches, factory gate meetings and demonstrations in places like Granby Street and the Market Square were common, with people rallying for change. Today, the legacy of Leicester's suffragettes is commemorated with a statue of Alice Hawkins in the Market Square, a tribute to her and all who fought for equality.

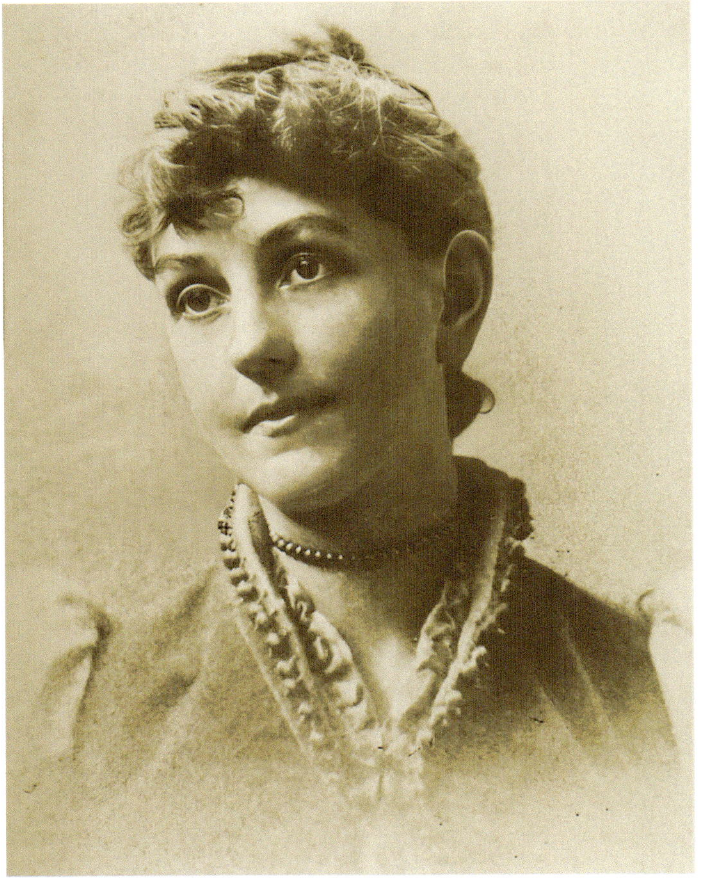

Nellie Taylor, a leading Leicester suffragette, and daughter of William Taylor, founder of optical lens company Taylor Hobson, later Rank Taylor Hobson.

7

Steam, Furnaces and Factories

While the steam engine stands as the defining innovation of the Industrial Revolution, powering factories, locomotives and ships, it was also a catalyst of a sweeping social revolution. By mechanising production and centralising it within purpose-built industrial facilities, the steam engine effectively dismantled the traditional cottage industries that had long sustained rural economies. This shift drew large numbers of workers into towns and cities where proximity to factories became essential.

As cities swelled with workers and their families, the demand for housing increased, leading to rapid and often haphazard inner-city residential development. These densely populated neighbourhoods strained existing infrastructure, placing pressure on basic services such as sanitation, clean water and waste disposal. Yet, paradoxically, the very technologies that drove industrial growth also enabled solutions to these urban challenges in the form of mass-produced iron pipework, steam-powered pumps and improved engineering practices that laid the groundwork for modern public health systems.

Socially, the Industrial Revolution reshaped class structures and community dynamics. The harsh conditions endured by workers, in mills, foundries and cramped living quarters, fostered a collective consciousness and a drive for solidarity. This gave rise to a range of grassroots movements and institutions: political organisations advocating for labour rights, friendly societies offering mutual aid, building societies facilitating home ownership and workers' co-operatives promoting shared economic benefit. These developments marked the emergence of a distinct working-class identity and laid the foundation for modern social reform and labour legislation.

In Leicester, these various movements had strong identities. Examples of their work remain today. The Wheatsheaf Works, built by the Co-operative Wholesale Society in 1891 still exists, but it is no longer a shoe factory. It was once the largest boot and shoe factory in the world and a flagship of co-operative industry. Today, the building is Grade II listed due to its architectural and historical significance. It has been converted into residential apartments, preserving much of its original Neo-Jacobean style and industrial character.

Co-operative Housing

A remarkable example of co-operative housing development in Leicester is the Humberstone Garden Suburb, established in the early twentieth century by the Anchor Boot and Shoe Co-operative Society. This initiative was directly inspired by the Garden City Movement, particularly the visionary ideas of Ebenezer Howard, which advocated for planned communities that harmoniously blended the advantages of urban and rural life.

The workers of the Anchor Co-operative Society played an active role in the suburb's creation, contributing a portion of their wages to collectively purchase land near the village of

Humberstone. Through this co-operative effort, they constructed ninety-seven houses, forming a community that embodied the principles of mutual aid and democratic participation.

The design of the Humberstone Garden Suburb reflected a conscious departure from the overcrowded and unsanitary conditions typical of inner-city housing at the time. It featured tree-lined streets, generous green spaces and individual homes with gardens, the hallmarks of the garden suburb ideal. This emphasis on healthier living conditions underscored the co-operative movement's broader commitment to social welfare and community well-being.

The development stands as a pioneering example of industrial workers extending their collective action beyond the workplace to shape their residential environment. It remains a significant part of Leicester's architectural and social history, demonstrating how co-operative principles can be applied not only to economic production but also to the creation of dignified and sustainable living spaces.

Nathaniel Corah

The Corah family had lived in Leicestershire since before 1600. Like many rural families, by the nineteenth century they made a living by combining framework knitting with farming. Nathaniel Corah, born in 1777, trained as a framesmith and, while still in his twenties, established a small textile business in Barlestone, north-west Leicestershire.

National recession forced Nathaniel into debt. Although he sought to negotiate and promised to pay back all the monies he owed, one of his creditors demanded his money. Nathaniel faced legal action and was imprisoned. On his release, anxious to pay his way, he became a worker in a gun factory in Birmingham.

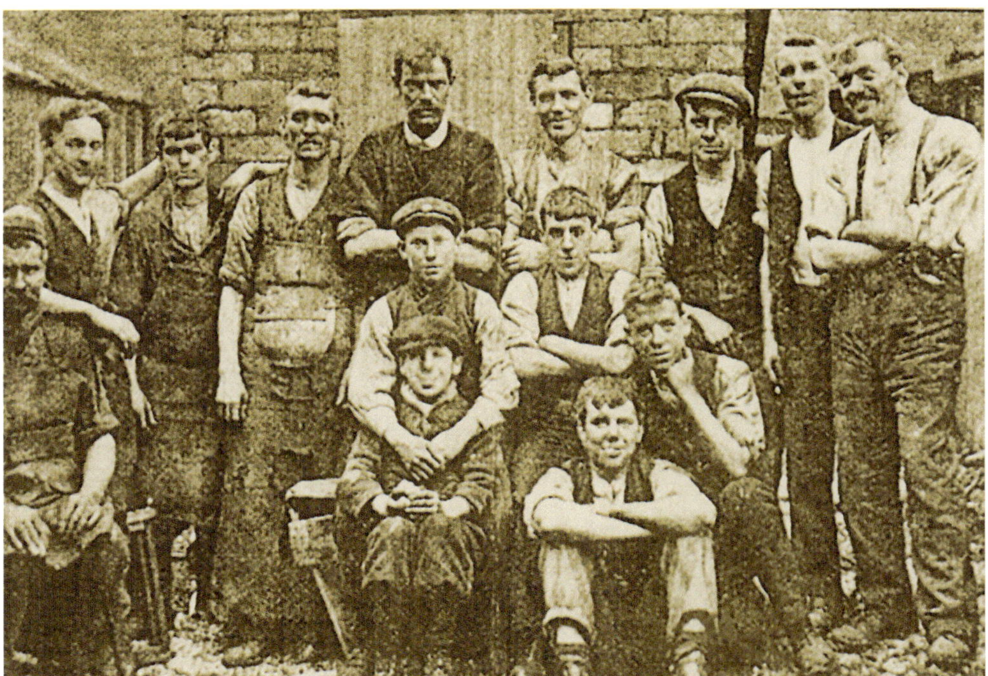

Henry Curry's first workers when his fledgling business began manufacturing bicycles.

Two years later, he was once again unemployed but had seen the potential for a new business. Whilst in prison, his wife and children had lived in Leicester. He saw there the expansion in the number of small stockingers and at the same time, the dramatic growth in the working-class population of Birmingham.

Corah began buying clothing from Leicester manufacturers, transporting it to Birmingham to be sold in markets. By personally selecting each item, he was able to maintain a high level of quality control which earned him a strong reputation among customers. On Saturday mornings, he bought goods offered at the Globe Inn on Leicester's Silver Street and then moved them to a small warehouse on Birmingham's Edgbaston Street.

The venture was very successful, and by 1824 Corah had acquired a block of buildings on Union Street, which he expanded in 1827. This gathering together of workers in a factory introduced the concept of organised production management to Leicester.

In 1830, Corah's sons, John, William and Thomas, joined the business which became Nathaniel Corah and Sons. This strategic move secured the firm's future because Nathaniel died just two years later at the age of fifty-one.

In his later, more prosperous years, Corah had repaid all but one of the debts that had once led to his imprisonment. He refused to settle the debt owed to the man who, in 1815, had ignored his pleas and insisted on his arrest.

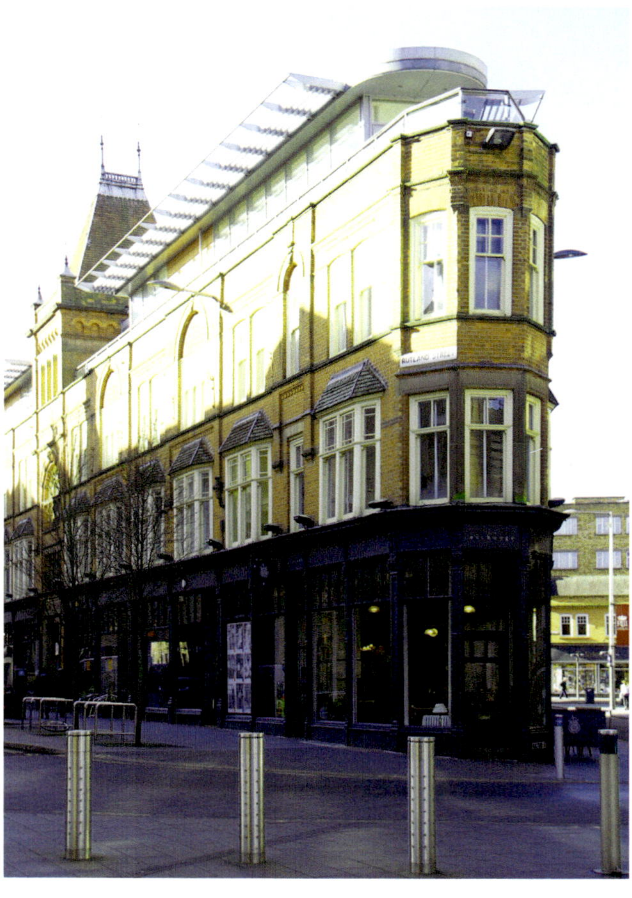

The Exchange or 'Flat Iron' building in Rutland Street, designed by Leicester architect Stockdale Harrison in 1922.

The next twenty years saw continued success for the company, its expansion prompting a move to a purpose-built factory in Granby Street and then to the famous St Margaret's works on a 4-acre site near St Margaret's Church. The foundation stone for this factory was laid by Edwin Corah, Thomas's son, on 13 July 1865, heralding the start of Corah's greatest years. Just one year later, St Margaret's works became the first textile factory in Leicester with integrated steam power when Edwin Corah's sister, Mennie Corah, formally fired up the company's beam engine.

By 1866, over 1,000 people were working at St Margaret's, and the buildings had been extended twice. The architect of the first part of the St Margaret's complex was William Jackson of Lowesby Lane in Leicester. Originally, a factory yard stretched north as far as the canal but by 1941 there had been no fewer than nineteen extensions to the original building, taking up all available land.

At the time of the move from Granby Street, the company had adopted an image of St Margaret as their emblem. A shepherdess martyred in AD 275, Margaret was a most appropriate symbol with her association with wool. The emblem was patented by the company on the very first day of the 1875 Trade Marks Registration Act and is therefore the oldest trade mark for knitted goods in the world. For many years, her statue, which some have said is weeping, stood proud on a plinth high on the external wall of the factory facing the present Vaughan Way. In the 1990s, after the

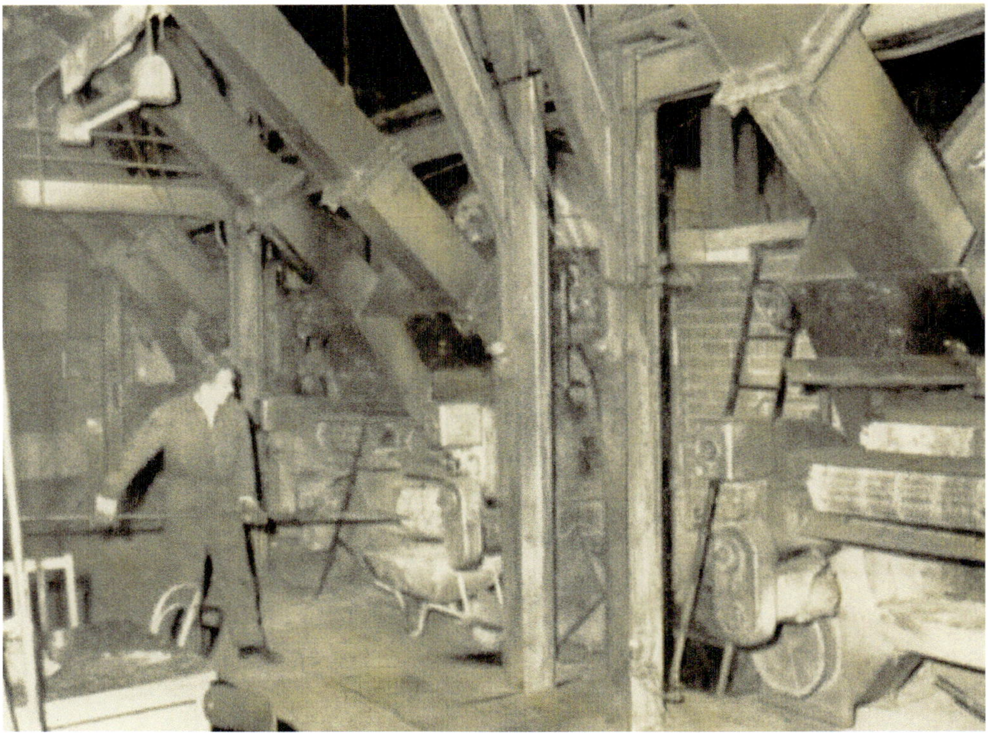

The boiler house of Nathaniel Corah's St Margaret's textile factory, where Henry Curry, founder of Curry's stores, once worked.

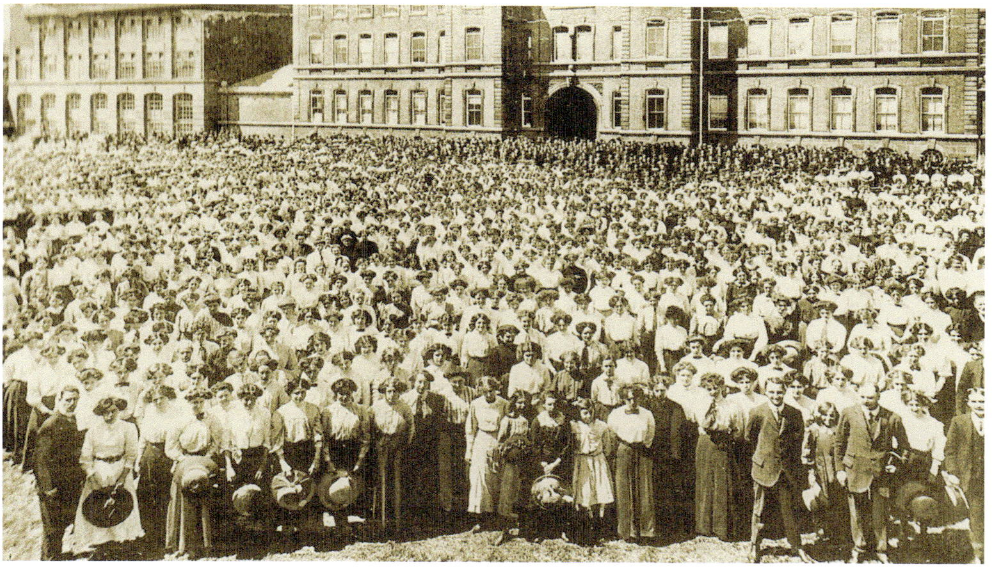

Exemplifying the dynamism of Leicester's textile industry in the nineteenth and twentieth centuries, Nathaniel Corah's workforce photographed in front of the St Margaret's factory frontage.

demise of the company and the sale of the buildings, the statue was removed, first to a location in the central courtyard, and then, in 2008, to St Margaret's Church facing St Margaret's Way.

True to the spirit of their founder, Corahs were pioneers. As well as being the first textile company to adopt production management and quality control, and the first to build a factory with integral steam-derived power, they were amongst the first to adopt new technical and managerial concepts. They were also the first textile firm in Leicester to install electric lighting, and the first in the country to give their workers a week's paid holiday every year. Corahs were always known as 'good' employers, an example to their competitors.

The Corah operation also provided training and social opportunities for its employees. For many, the company was their escape' from the confines of their small family homes and became an opportunity to socialise beyond their immediate neighbours.

One of the most well-known former employees of the firm was Henry Curry, an apprentice in the steam engine house at St Margaret's. The skills he learned in machining and welding enabled him later to establish his own bicycle manufacturing business working initially from a shed in the back garden of his family home and then from premises in Belgrave Gate near to the clock tower. From this small enterprise grew the Curry's national electrical retail chain which continued to manufacture and sell bicycles into the 1960s and is still at the forefront of British retail.

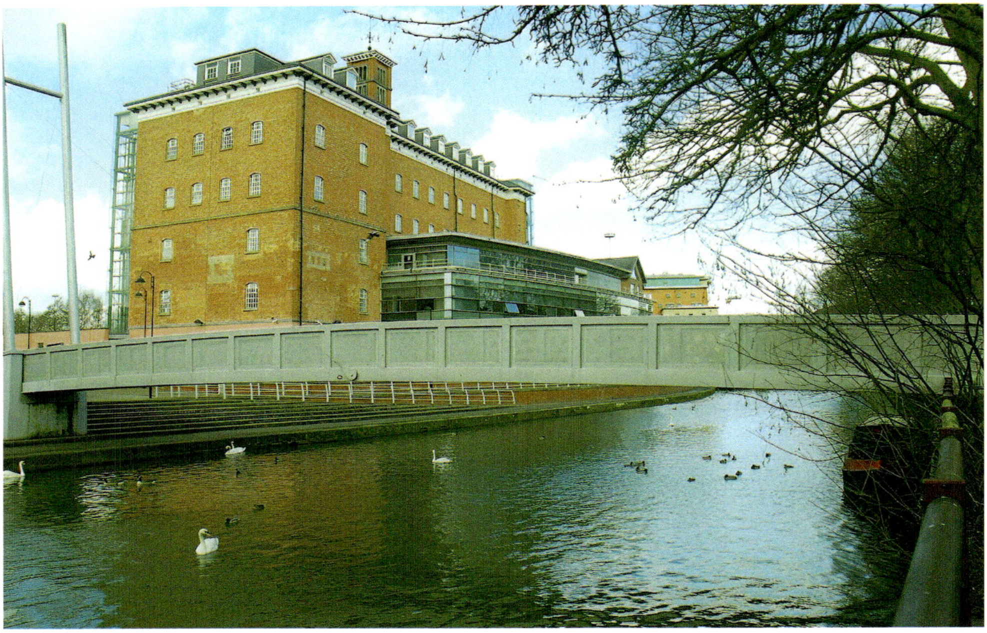

The former Westbridge Mill, now a modern office amenity in the heart of Leicester.

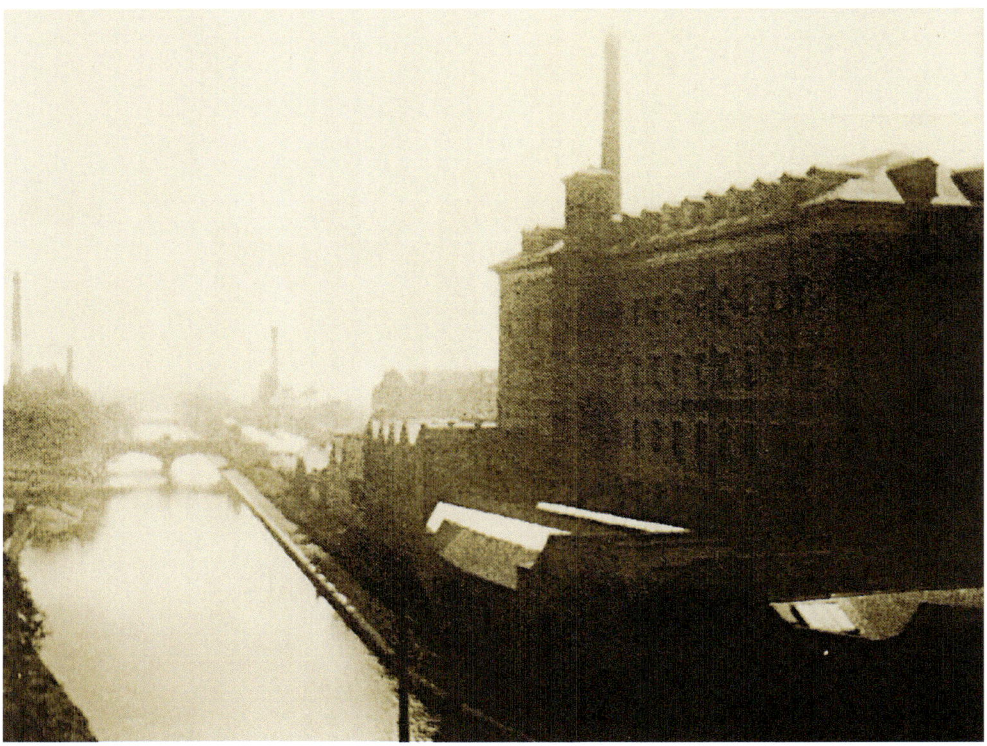

The Westbridge Mill when industry was still dominant along the riverside. This photograph was by George Moore Henton.

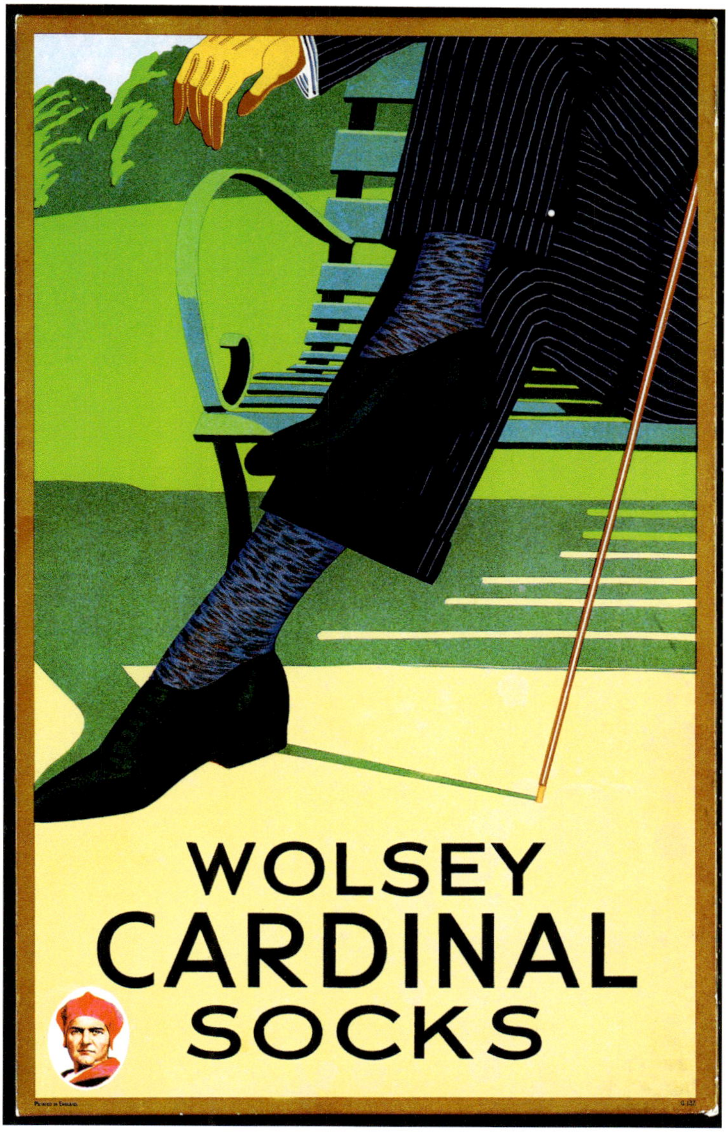

A poster advertising socks made by Wolsey Knitwear, Leicester's oldest textile brand.

The Moira Furnace

The construction of beam engines and equipment for producing hosiery and textiles was made possible by the building of iron furnaces to smelt iron. The first in Leicestershire was the Moira Furnace, constructed in 1804 by Francis Rawdon Hastings, the 2nd Earl of Moira. He built it to capitalise on the rich deposits of iron ore and coal which he owned in north-west Leicestershire. The site was strategically chosen for its proximity to the Ashby-de-la-Zouch Canal, facilitating the efficient transportation of materials and goods. It was fuelled by coke and employed a steam engine to create the blast. However, despite its innovative design, it was a commercial failure and only operated intermittently between 1806 and 1811.

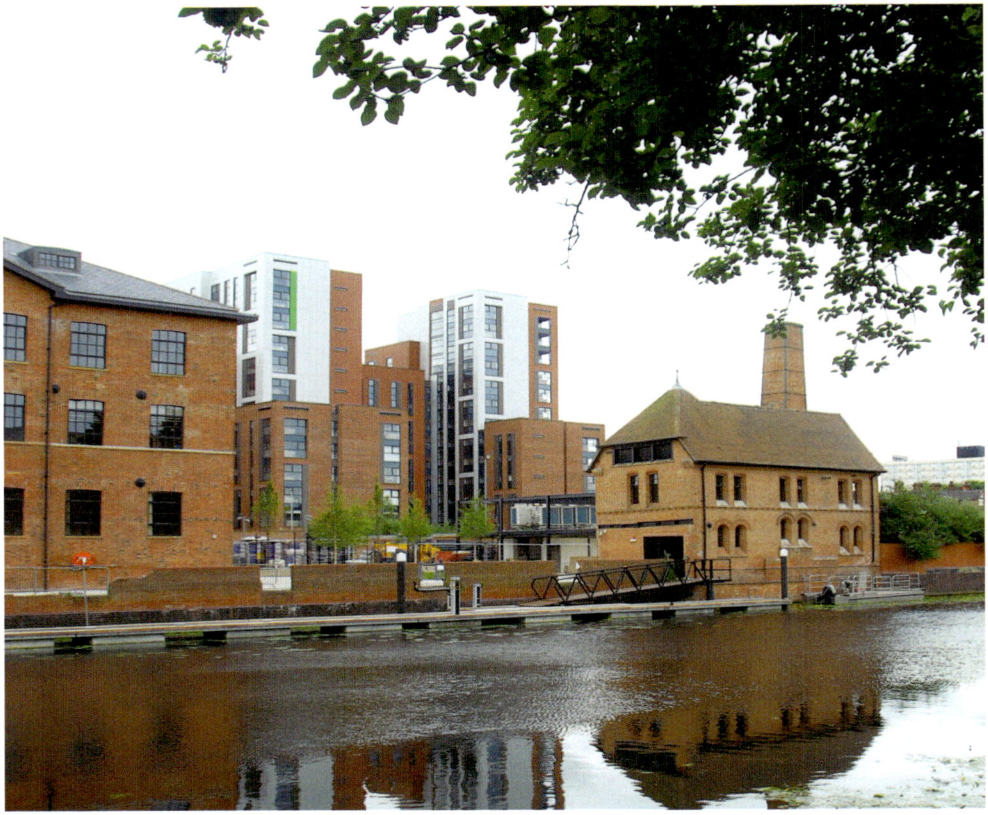

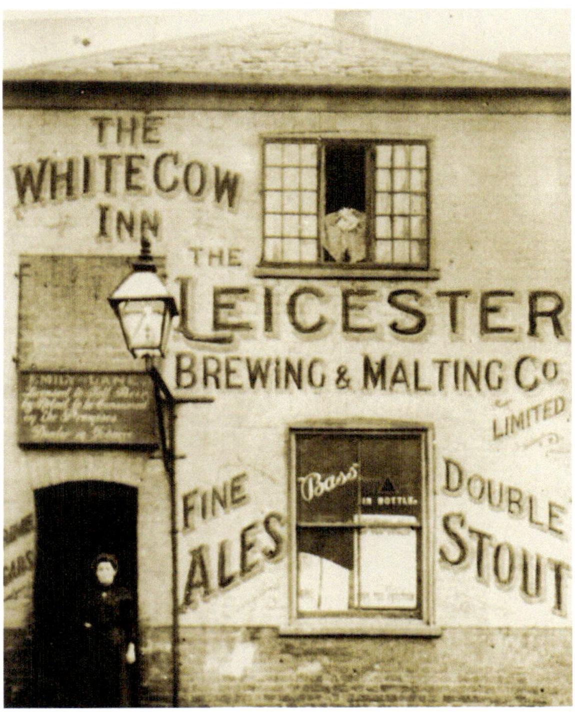

Above: Built in 1739, Friars Mill, known locally as the Donisthorpe Mill, is Leicester's oldest surviving factory building.

Left: The White Cow stood at the corner of Russell Square and Willow Bridge Street in one of the poorest areas of the town. It closed in 1907.

Gimson

The Gimson Foundry, formally known as Gimson and Company, was a cornerstone of Leicester's industrial development during the nineteenth and early twentieth centuries. Founded in 1840 by brothers Benjamin and Josiah Gimson, the company began on Welford Road and quickly established itself as a leading manufacturer of steam engines, ironwork and machinery for the footwear and agricultural industries.

In response to growing demand, the firm expanded significantly between 1876 and 1879, constructing the Vulcan Works on Humberstone Road, one of the earliest British industrial complexes to integrate an iron foundry with an engineering works.

The Vulcan Works was an impressive facility, designed by local architect John Breedon Everard, and featured a three-storey building with a 120-foot chimney and direct access to the Midland Railway. By the 1880s, Gimson and Company employed several hundred workers and became one of Leicester's largest employers. The company was also notable for its progressive labour practices, with Josiah Gimson advocating for fair working conditions and supporting the movement for a nine-hour working day.

Gimson's engineering legacy includes large beam engines, several of which are preserved at sites including the Abbey Pumping Station in Leicester and Claymills Pumping Station in Burton-on-Trent.

Although the company ceased manufacturing at Vulcan Road in 1986, the historic building was later refurbished and now serves as the Vulcan House Business Centre, preserving its architectural heritage while adapting to modern commercial use.

Ernest William Gimson, born in Leicester in 1864, was a leading figure in the English Arts and Crafts movement and the son of Josiah Gimson. Although Ernest chose not to follow his father into the industrial business, his upbringing in a household deeply engaged with engineering and craftsmanship profoundly shaped his artistic philosophy.

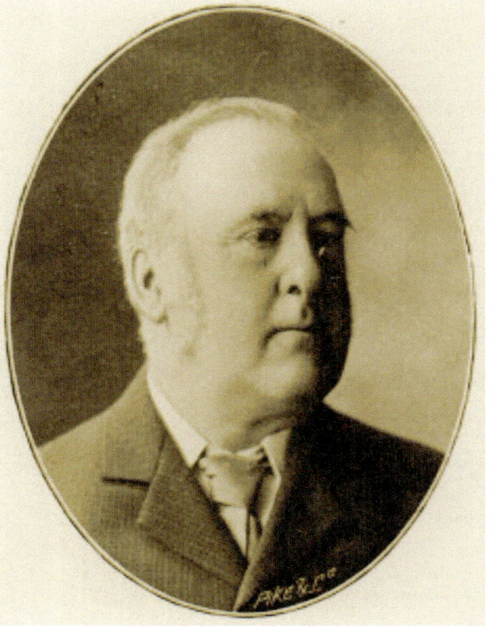

Thomas Fielding Johnson (1828–1921), a prominent businessman and philanthropist, in 1919 donated land and buildings to establish a college which became Leicester University.

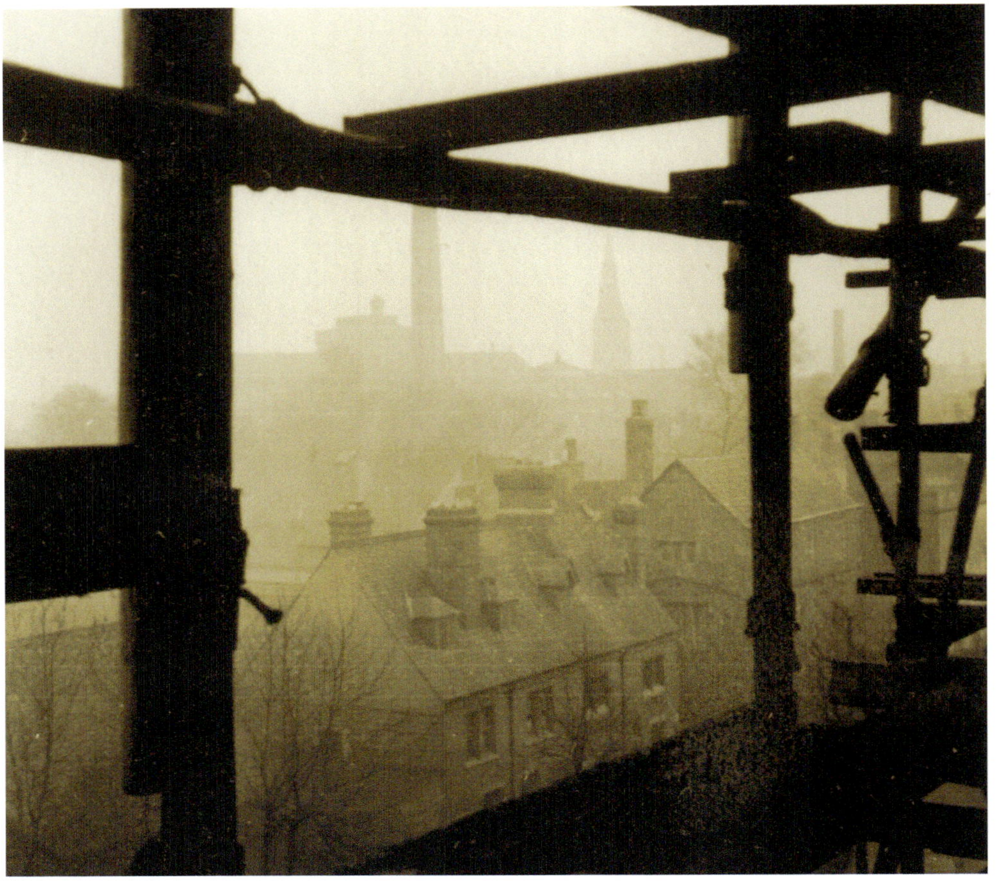

An aerial view of Leicester from the Newarke in April 1936. The cathedral spire is prominent in the background.

He was articled to the arts and crafts architect Isaac Barradale in Leicester and later moved to London where he was inspired by William Morris and immersed himself in the ideals of the Arts and Crafts movement.

Gimson's work was characterised by a commitment to traditional craftsmanship, natural materials and harmonious design. He became renowned for his furniture, architecture and plasterwork, often collaborating with skilled artisans to realise his vision. His designs rejected industrial mass production in favour of hand-crafted quality, a stance that contrasted with the mechanised output of his father's foundry but was nonetheless rooted in the same respect for skilled labour and material integrity. His legacy lives on in the buildings he designed, such as Stoneywell in Leicestershire, and in the continued appreciation of Arts and Crafts furniture.

Leicester Clothing the World

In the nineteenth century, Leicester emerged as a dynamic hub of manufacturing and technological innovation, playing a pivotal role in Britain's industrial expansion. The city's economy was dominated by a diverse array of industries, with textiles and footwear

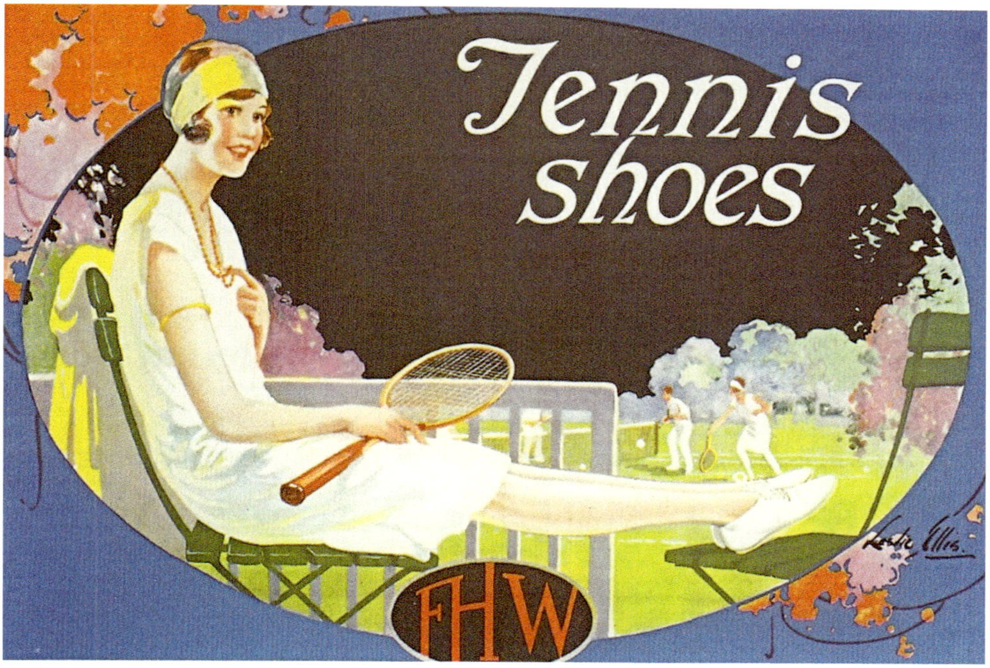

A poster advertising Freeman Hardy Willis tennis shoes, stylish and contemporary with its time.

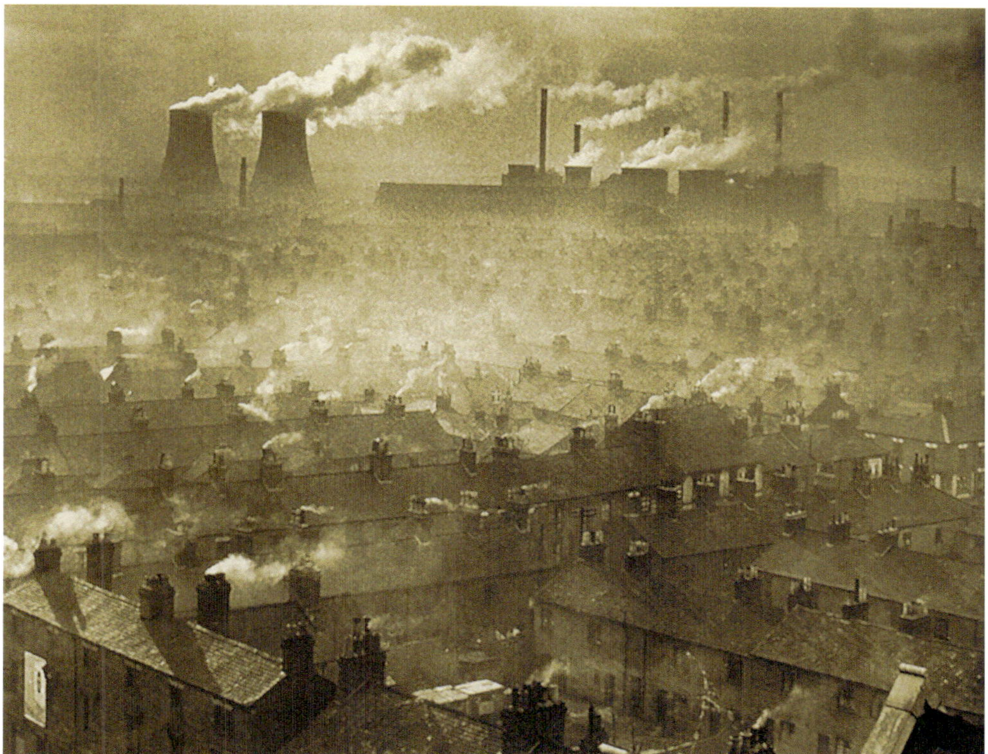

Leicester during the era when coal was king.

at the forefront. Renowned textile firms such as Corah, Wolsey and Kemptons became household names, producing vast quantities of knitwear, hosiery and garments that were distributed across the country, sold under the top retail brands such as Marks and Spencer and exported abroad. These companies not only drove economic growth but also shaped Leicester's identity as a centre of craftsmanship and industrial excellence.

The hosiery sector flourished with companies like Byfords, which specialised in high-quality socks and undergarments, contributing to Leicester's reputation for fine knitwear. Meanwhile, the boot and shoe industry thrived with manufacturers such as Liberty Shoes, which provided durable and stylish footwear to a growing consumer base.

Supporting these industries were the engineering firms that supplied the machinery essential for mass production. The leader in this field was the British United Shoe Machinery Company (BUSMC) which became a global leader in shoe-making equipment. In the 1960s it was Leicester's largest employer with over 4,500 local staff and 9,500 worldwide.

The company began with a small factory belonging to Joseph Merry and Charles Bennion in Wharf Street in the 1870. Following Merry's death, Bennion formed a new partnership in 1898 with Marshall Pearson and moved into new premises in Belgrave Road. The company expanded rapidly and three years later bought 10 acres of land to extend the works. Bennion later purchased Bradgate Park for the people of Leicester not long before his death in 1929.

Together, these enterprises formed an industrial network that powered Leicester's economy, transformed its urban landscape, and laid the foundations for social and cultural development. The city's factories and workshops were more than places of work; they were engines of innovation, community, and progress.

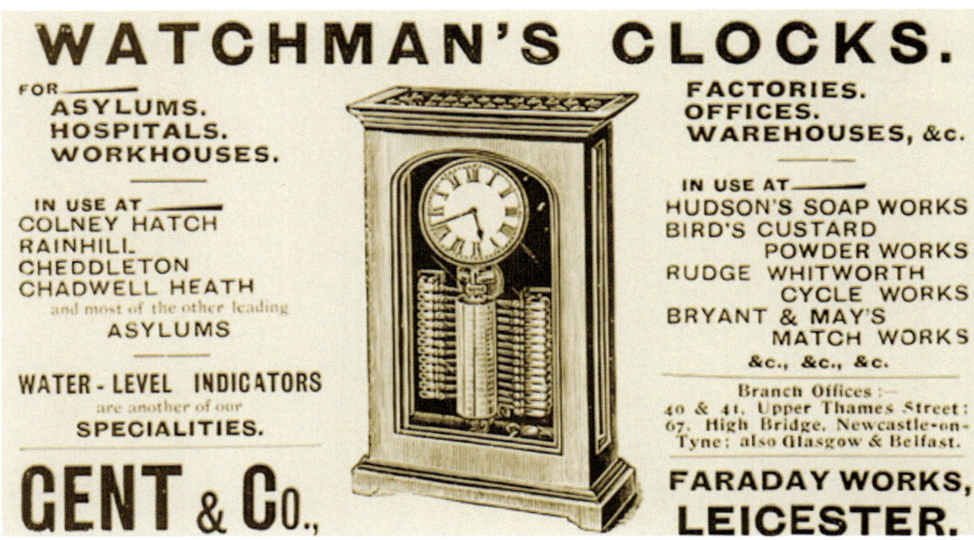

An advertisement for Gent's watchman's clocks which were used in factories and public buildings across the country.

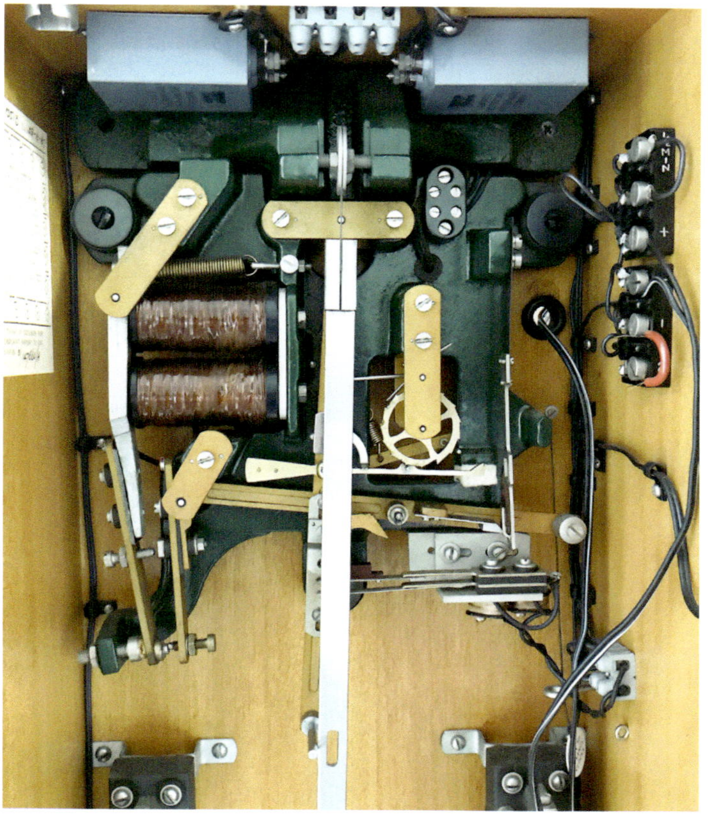

The control mechanism of a Gent's Pulsynetic clock, known as a 'waiting train'.

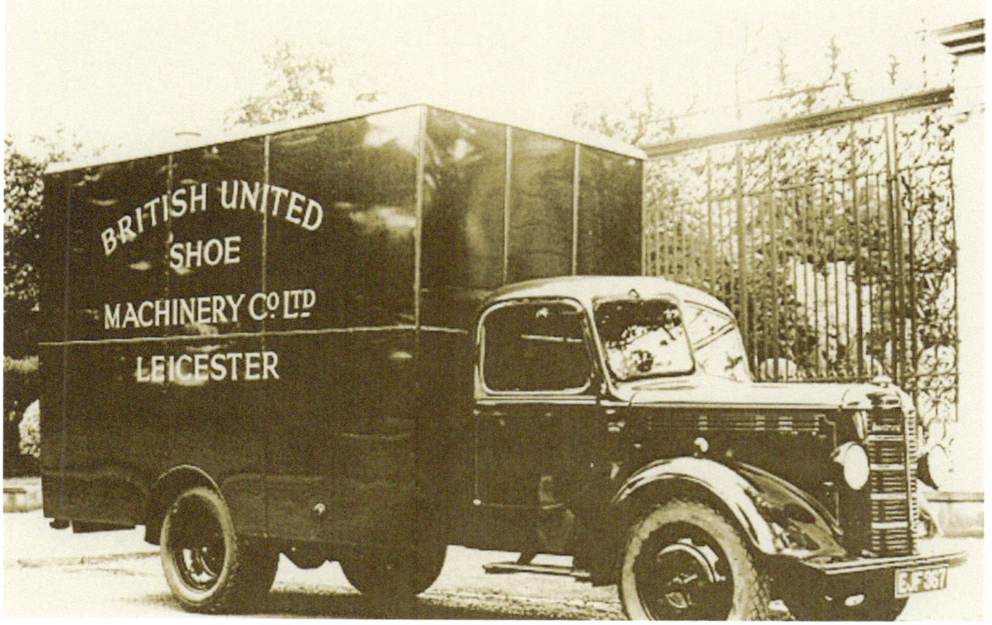

Leicester's British United Shoe Machinery Company distributed their products worldwide. However, this vehicle is parked up outside the gates to Victoria Park!

8

Health, Wealth and Public Buildings

The architects, businessmen and philanthropists of the Victorian era created the urban landscape of our towns and cities and influenced their character. In Leicester, after more than a century of demolition and reconstruction, Victorian facades still prevail throughout the city centre and outwards into the residential suburbs. Even where ground-floor facades have been modernised, as in Gallowtree Gate, Belgrave Gate and High Street, the first-floor Victorian façades often remain.

In the centre of Leicester, the Victorians built their factories and mills, churches, hotels, railway stations, libraries, wholesale market, police and fire stations and, of course, the Town Hall. On the outskirts were the isolation hospitals, the workhouse and sewerage works, as well as the signature residences of the wealthier citizens. Rarely were any of these edifices modest in scale or design; the message in the brickwork, stone and mortar was of wealth, often on a grand scale. The Grand Hotel in Granby Street is a fine example.

The Victorians' sense of architectural grandeur extended to their philanthropic activities. Thomas Cook, a lifelong supporter of the temperance movement, became a founding member

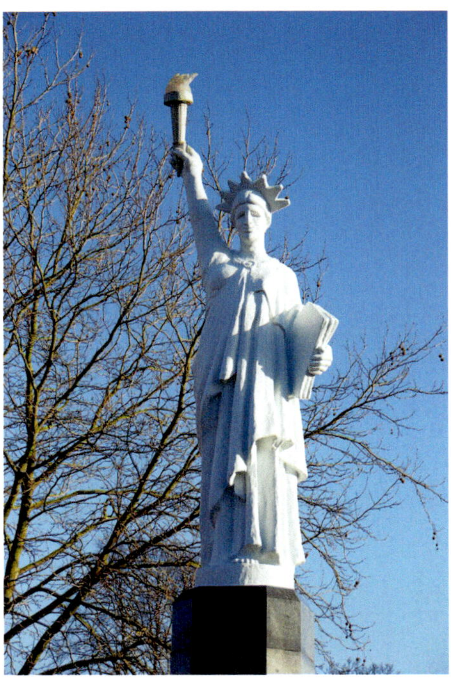

The Liberty Statue, created by Leicester stonemason Joseph Morcom in 1919. It stood on the roof of the Liberty Shoes factory until it was demolished in 2003. It was then moved to the centre of the nearby roundabout.

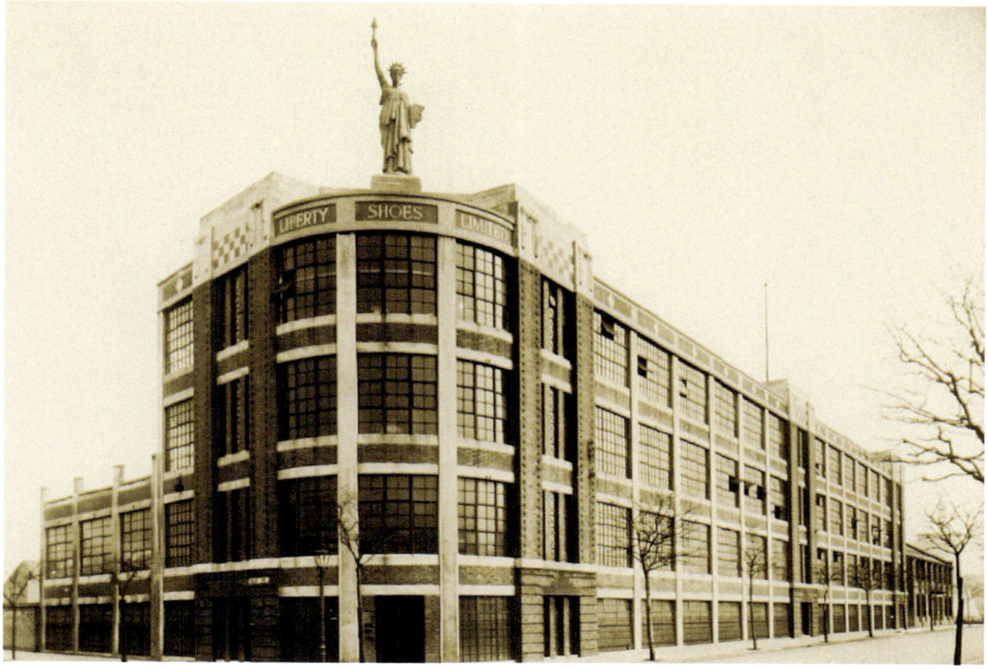

The former Lennards' Liberty Shoes factory on Eastern Boulevard with the Statue of Liberty on the roof.

of the Leicester Coffee and Cocoa Company Ltd in 1877. The company aimed to provide refreshment by establishing coffee houses, rooms, carts and stalls throughout Leicester.

Many working men lived in suburban areas but worked in the town centre and often took their lunch breaks in public houses. The coffee houses offered an affordable and healthier option, serving hot meals such as a large basin of nourishing soup for two pence and drinks for a penny a pint. These venues were designed to be bright, attractive and comfortable social spaces where both men and women could relax, read newspapers and enjoy amusements. Some included ladies' rooms or billiards rooms.

The coffee houses were respected for their spaciousness, cleanliness and order, qualities previously only found at high prices. When the Victoria Coffee House opened in 1888, the Duchess of Rutland commended the directors for combining commercial success with public benefit. She noted that people across the country were eager to learn how Leicester's coffee houses had achieved such remarkable success. Ultimately, the company established fourteen coffee houses in the town.

Most premises were custom-built and designed by architect Edward Burgess, a local Quaker. Several notable examples still stand today, though they serve different purposes. The East Gates Coffee House, Church Gate (1885), was opened by the Duchess of Rutland and was admired for its fifteenth-century domestic style. It provided a popular and profitable service for over forty years before closing shortly after the First World War. The Victoria House in Granby Street (1887) was built to honour Queen Victoria's Golden Jubilee. This five-storey turreted building in the French Renaissance style was considered the finest coffee house in the country.

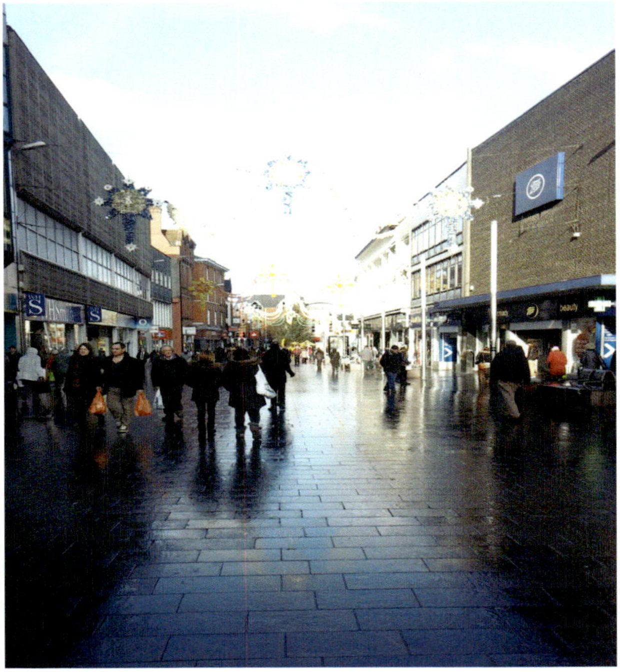

Gallowtree Gate, looking towards the clock tower in December 2014.

The Town Hall

Leicester's Town Hall stands out as a notable exception among the city's civic buildings. Tucked away from the city's main thoroughfares in a quiet, almost secluded location, once the site of the town's bustling cattle market, it exudes a calm and dignified presence. The building is graceful but understated, reflecting civic pride and authority without ostentation. Unlike the grand, imposing – and sometimes gaunt – town halls found in many northern cities, ours is built from warm Ketton stone and harmonises with its surroundings rather than dominating them.

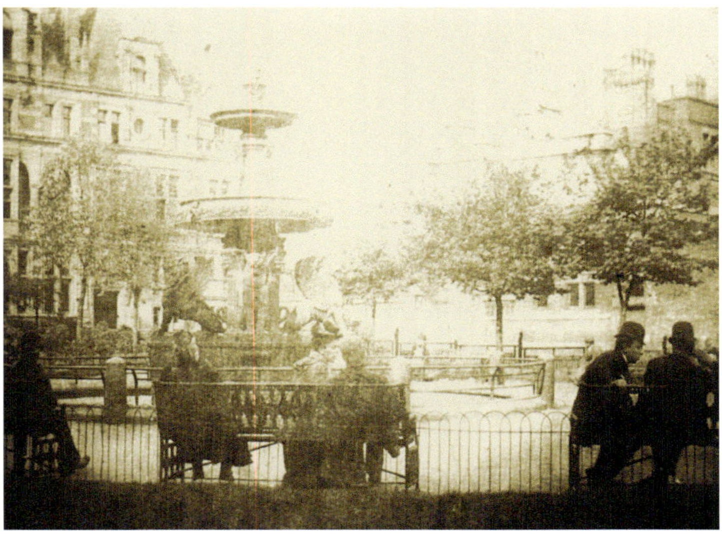

An early photograph of people meeting and relaxing in Town Hall Square, from a glass slide dating to the 1870s.

It was designed by local architect Francis J. Hames in the Queen Anne style. Construction began with the laying of the foundation stone on 3 August 1874, and the building was officially opened on 7 August 1876 by Mayor Alderman William Barfoot. The clock tower topped with a cupola stands 44 metres above the road level. It replaced the medieval Guildhall which had become inadequate for the city's growing administrative needs. The new building housed council offices, law courts, a sanitary department, a school board and even police cells in the basement. The adjacent square and its ornamental fountain, also designed by Hames, were added later.

The Clock Tower

The Haymarket Memorial Clock Tower in Leicester is one of the city's most iconic landmarks and a central meeting point for generations of local people. Completed in 1868, it was built on the site of the former hay and straw market to address traffic congestion at the intersection of the five busy streets: Gallowtree Gate, Humberstone Gate, Haymarket, Church Gate and Eastgates.

The idea for the clock tower was championed by John Burton, a local photographer and publisher, whose premises were close to the clock tower site. He led a public campaign to make the area a safer and more attractive civic space. A fundraising effort in 1867 saw 472 subscribers contribute £872, with the remaining funds provided by the Corporation of Leicester.

Designed by local architect Joseph Goddard, with sculptures by Samuel Barfield of Kibworth, the tower was constructed using Ketton limestone, with a granite base and

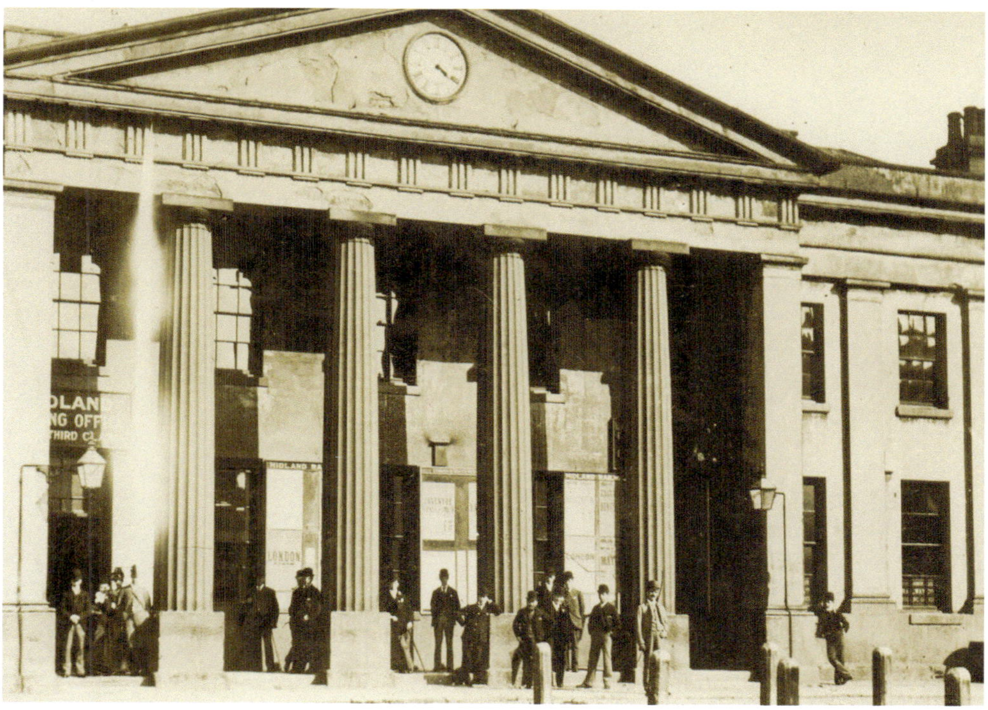

The impressive facade of the Campbell Street railway station, demolished in 1892.

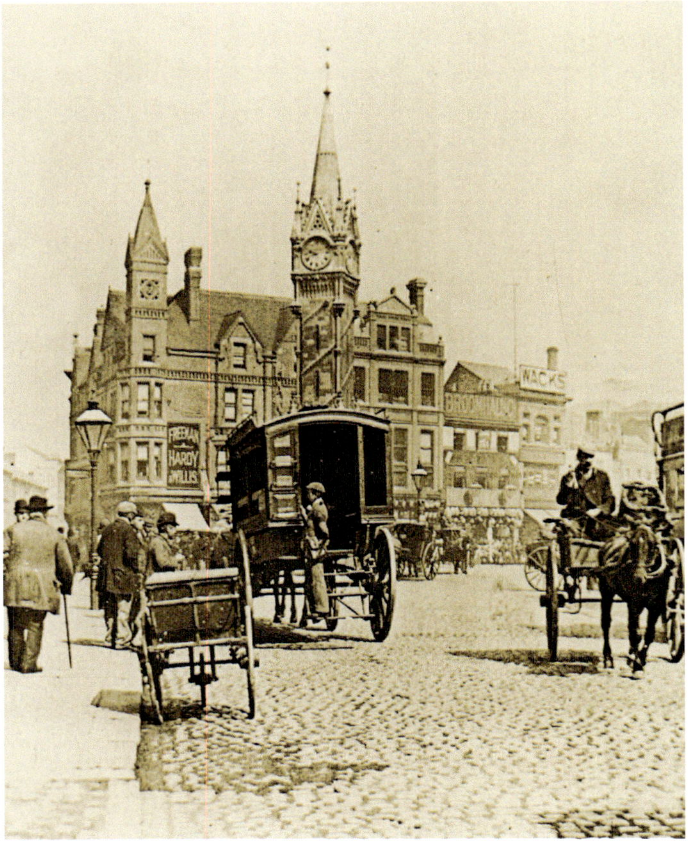

Leicester's Memorial Clock Tower, photographed in 1895, three years after its construction.

decorative statues made of Portland stone. The four statues commemorate notable figures in Leicester's history: Simon de Montfort, William Wigston, Sir Thomas White and Alderman Gabriel Newton.

Originally conceived as the first traffic island in Britain, the clock tower became a focal point of civic pride. It was surrounded by tramlines in 1903, forming one of the most complex junctions in the country. Later, being the intersection of several streets carrying an increased number of vehicles, the clock tower was bypassed by the creation of Charles Street, which, in turn, was bypassed by St Matthew's Way, part of the Inner Ring.

Joseph Gordon: A Pioneering Force in Leicester's Public Health

Joseph Gordon, originally from Haltwhistle in Northumberland, played a pivotal yet often overlooked role in transforming public health in Leicester. After gaining experience in Germany on major urban sanitation projects, he was appointed Borough Surveyor for Leicester in 1881.

At the time, Leicester faced a severe public health crisis. The town had the highest infant mortality rate among large English towns, mainly due to sewage-related pollution. Sewerage waste was transported by rail or canal and discharged into the River Soar, causing significant contamination. In 1884, a government inspector described the river's condition in Belgrave as 'most deplorable'.

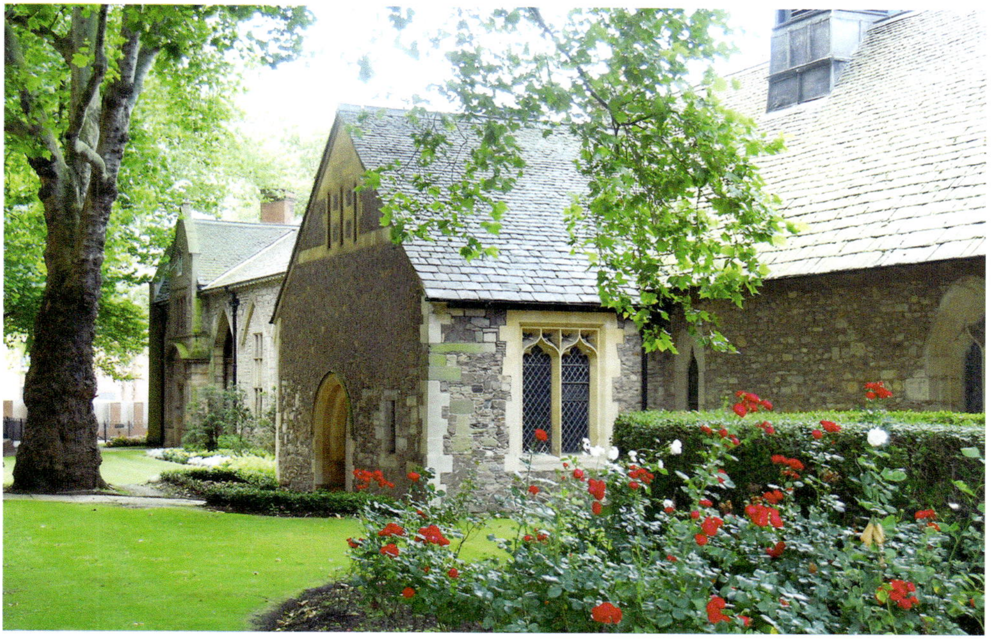

Trinity House. Formerly Trinity Hospital, now housing De Montfort University's administrative offices.

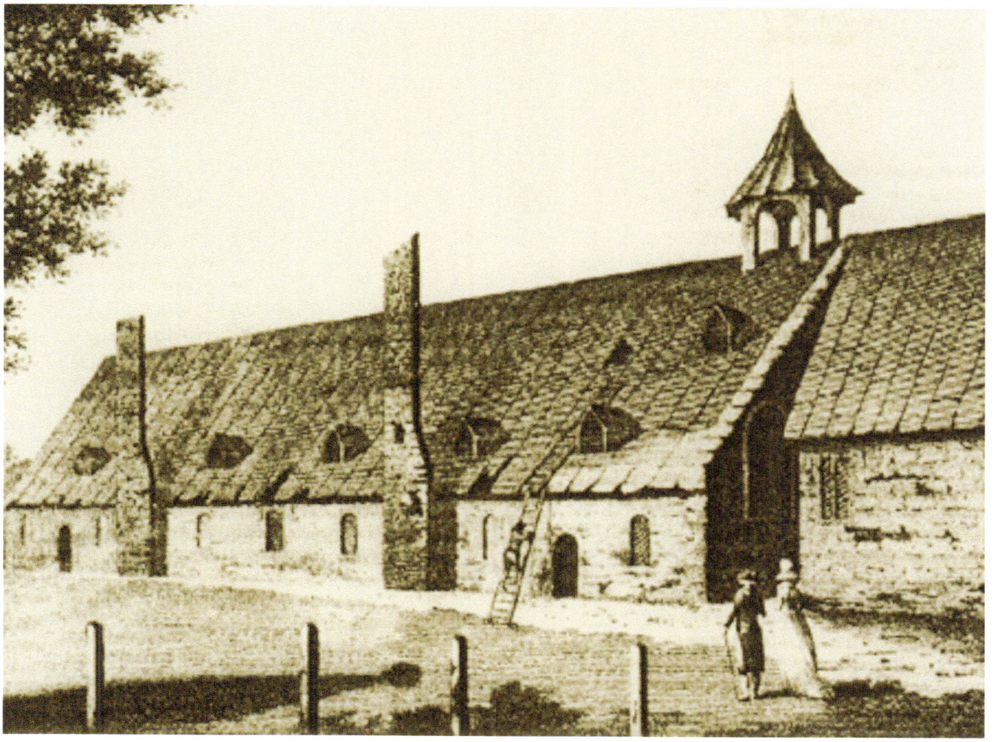

Trinity Hospital, Leicester' oldest care charity, was founded in 1330 by Henry Plantagenet, 3rd Earl of Leicester.

Gordon led a major civil engineering initiative that revolutionised the town's sanitation infrastructure. His work included the creation of a new sewer system, the establishment of the Beaumont Leys sewage farm and the construction of the Abbey Pumping Station.

Designed by local architect Stockdale Harrison, the pumping station featured four massive steam engines built by Gimsons of Leicester. Costing the Corporation £22,269, equivalent to over £2 million today, the engines were able to pump twenty million gallons of sewage daily. They operated continuously for seventy-three years until their decommissioning in 1964. Two main sewers serviced the station. One ran from the east of the town beneath Bruin Street and the Grand Union Canal, and another ran along Abbey Lane across the Abbey meadows.

Gordon's sanitation reforms had a profound impact, dramatically reducing infant mortality rates in Leicester to close to the national average. His system was designed with future expansion in mind, and by 1912, an additional 130 miles of sewers had been installed. The Beaumont Leys sewage farm remained in operation until the 1970s when it was replaced by the Wanlip Sewerage Treatment Plant.

Gordon's expertise earned him national recognition. He became President of the Association of Municipal and County Engineers and was appointed Chief Engineer for the London County Council in 1889. Tragically, he fell ill shortly after taking up that post and died in November of that year at the age of fifty-two. He is buried in Welford Road Cemetery.

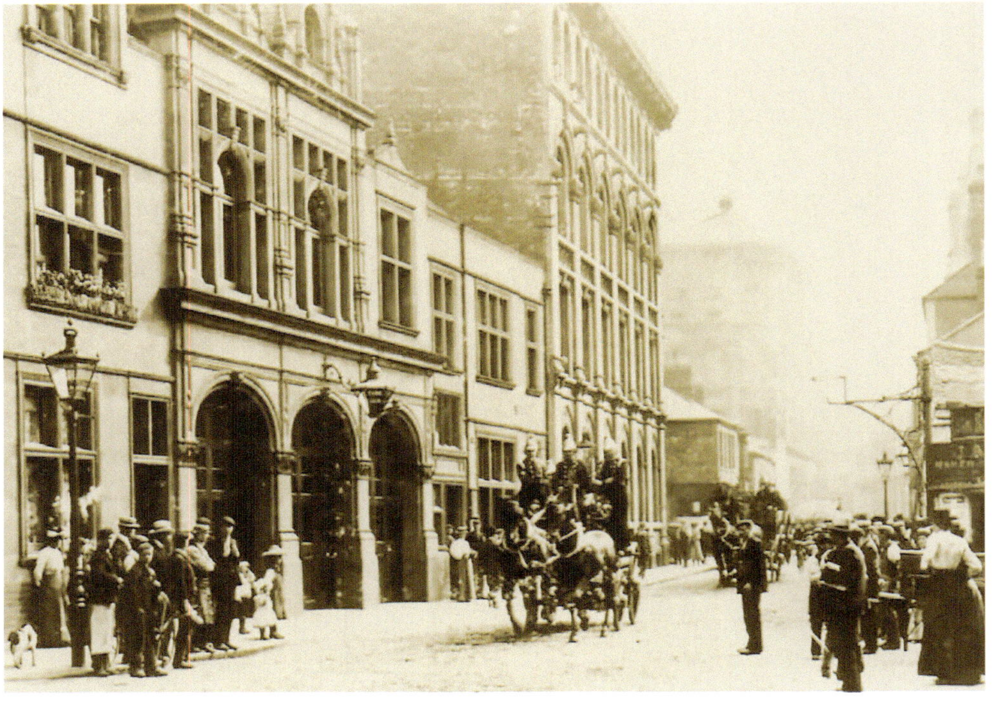

Leicester's fire brigade returning to their Rutland Street station after attending a fire. This was their base from 1892 until the 1920s.

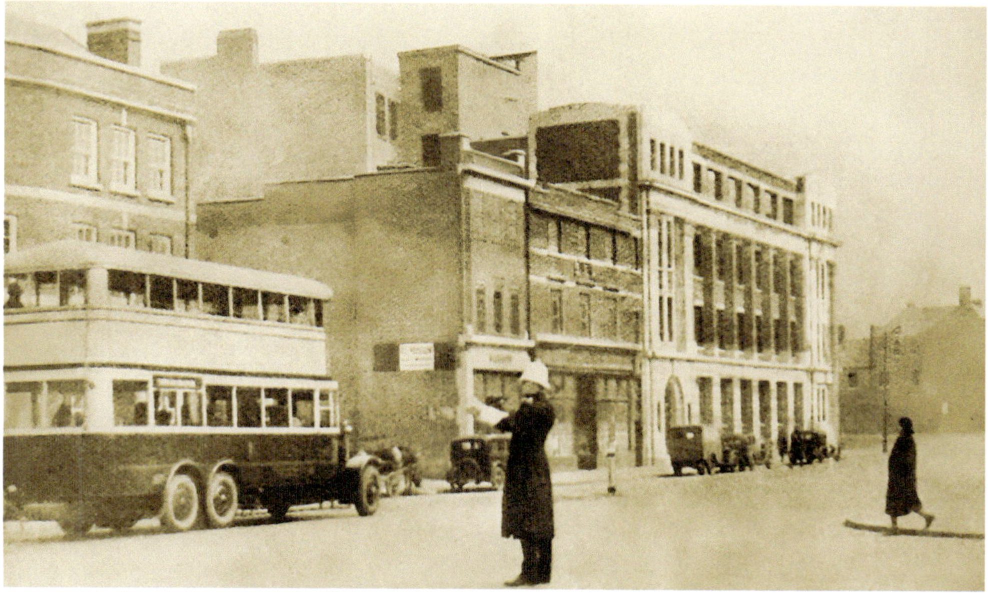

Charles Street in 1932. The building behind the bus is now the Ale Wagon pub.

Law and Order

In the nineteenth century, Leicester experienced significant changes in its approach to policing and maintaining law and order, largely driven by industrialisation and related

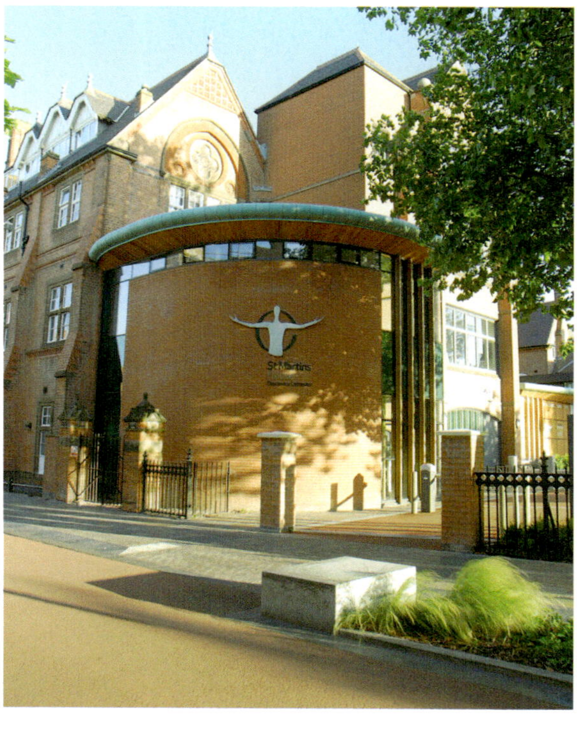

The former Wyggeston Boys' School, now St Martin's House.

social unrest. Before 1836, the town relied on informal systems of night watchmen and day police appointed by the borough corporation. This changed with the Municipal Corporations Act of 1835, which required towns to establish formal police forces. Leicester responded by creating the Leicester Borough Police in January 1836, initially comprising one inspector, five sergeants and forty-five constables. Their headquarters was first located in the medieval Guildhall before moving to the Town Hall in 1875.

Frederick Goodyer, formerly of the Metropolitan Police, was appointed as Leicester's first Chief Constable. He was instrumental in organising the new force and managing public order during periods of significant unrest, including the activities of local members of the Chartist movement. His leadership was noted for its effectiveness and restraint, particularly during large public gatherings and protests.

Further Education

De Montfort University traces its origins back to the founding of the Leicester School of Art in 1870. Established in response to a growing demand for skilled workers in local industries such as textiles, furniture making and printing, the school began with classes held in a disused warehouse on Pocklington's Walk. Over the following decades, it expanded its curriculum to include technical subjects including engineering and architecture, reflecting the industrial needs of the time.

In 1897, the Leicester School of Art merged with the Leicester Technical School to form the Leicester Municipal Technical and Art School, which later evolved into the Leicester Colleges of Art and Technology. This institution became Leicester Polytechnic in 1969 and finally gained university status in 1992 under the name of De Montfort University.

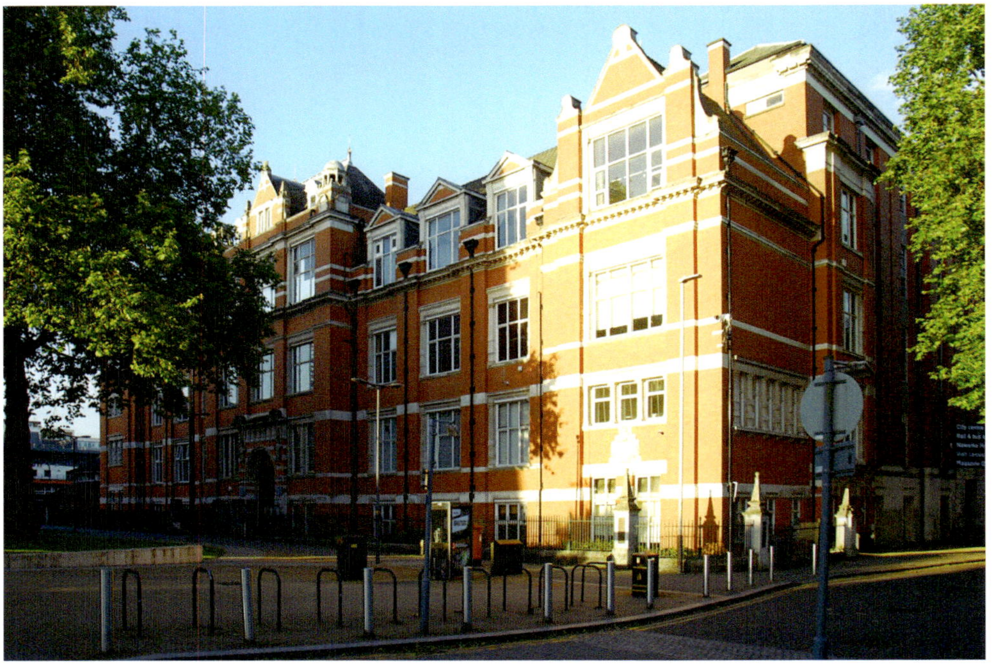

The Hawthorn Building in the Newarke, formerly the home of the Leicester School of Art.

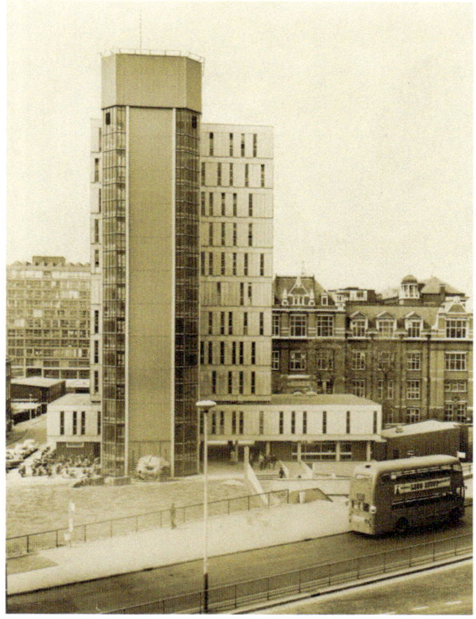

Right: The James Went Building on the Newarke Campus of De Montfort University, overshadowing the Hawthorn Building. Built in 1969, it was demolished in 2005.

Below: Two of the thousands of participants in the Leicester Pageant, which took place over ten days in June 1932, taking a break to read the *Evening Mail.*

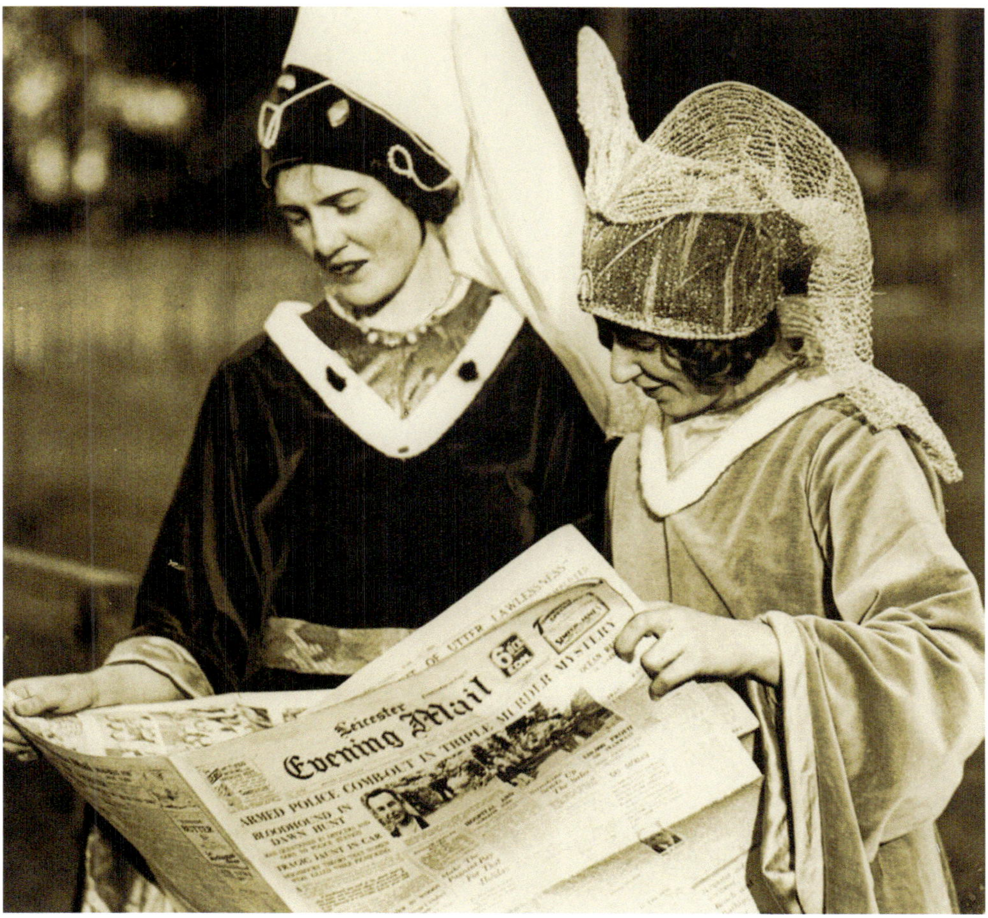

Vaughan College in Leicester began in 1862 as the Working Men's Institute, founded by Revd David Vaughan, vicar of St Martin's parish, to provide evening education for working-class men. Inspired by London's Working Men's College, the institute offered classes in reading, writing and other subjects, later expanding to include women in 1880, thanks in part to the efforts of Vaughan's wife, Margaret.

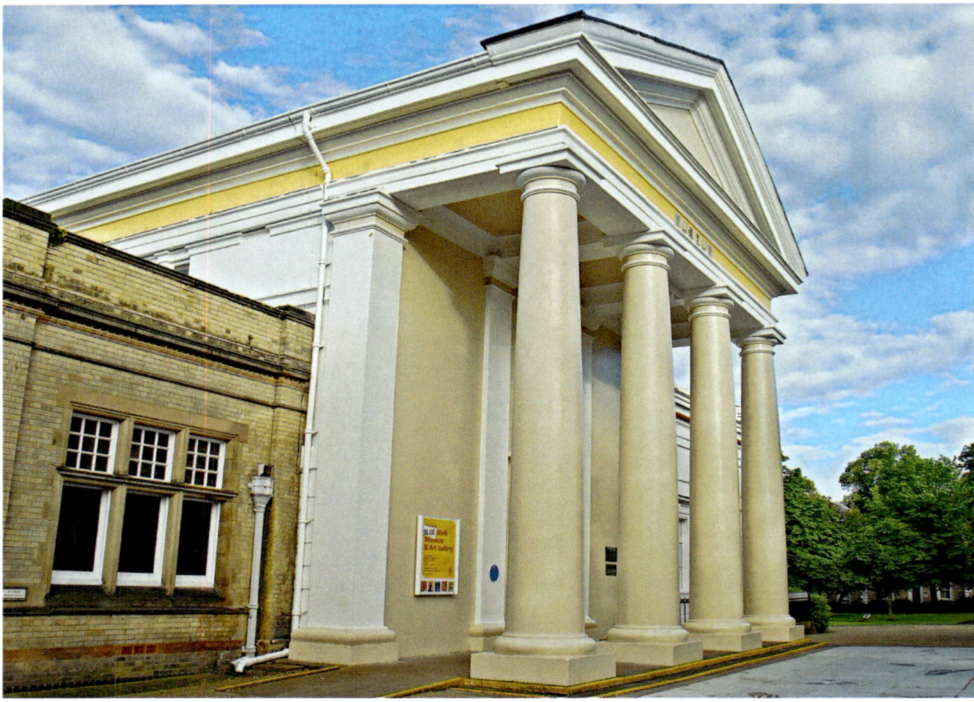

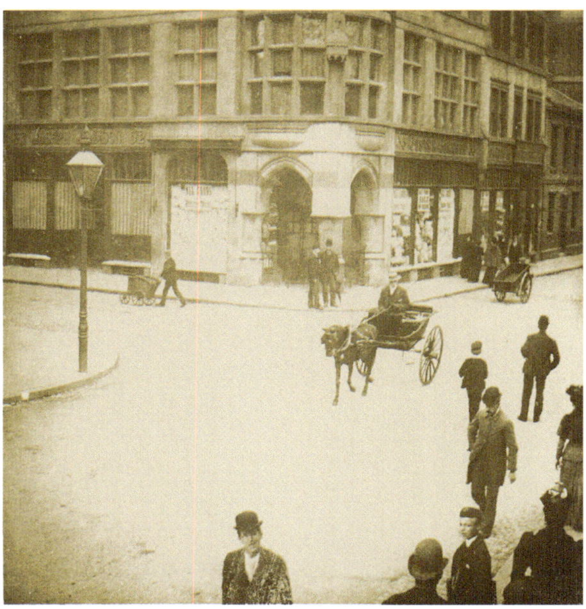

Above: The New Walk Museum and Art Gallery, built as the New Walk Proprietary School in 1836. Visits to the museum as a boy inspired Sir David Attenborough to study natural history.

Left: The former Joseph Johnson department store, photographed in the 1870s. From 1962, it was occupied by Fenwicks and is now an aparthotel and restaurant.

In 1908, the college moved into its own building on Great Central Street, becoming the Vaughan Working Men's College, the only provincial institution of its kind to survive into the twentieth century. In 1929, Vaughan College merged with University College, Leicester, becoming its extramural department and continuing to offer adult education, including part-time and degree-level courses.

A Powerful Legacy

The Victorian era, marked by Queen Victoria's reign, was a period of profound transformation in Britain. Health saw significant advancements with the rise of public health initiatives, improved sanitation and the founding of modern hospitals, though urban overcrowding and disease remained challenges. Philanthropy flourished, driven by religious and moral motivations, with wealthy industrialists and reformers funding schools, orphanages and charitable organizations. Business and enterprise thrived amid the Industrial Revolution, which spurred innovation, mass production and the expansion of railways and global trade. This era also witnessed the rise of a powerful middle class and a strong work ethic, underpinned by Victorian values of progress, self-improvement and social responsibility.

However, the Victorian age was also marked by stark social inequality. While the upper and middle classes enjoyed increasing prosperity, the working classes often lived in squalid conditions, enduring long hours in factories, mines and mills for meagre wages. Child labour was widespread, and many families relied on every member, including children, to contribute to household income. Despite these hardships, the working class developed strong community bonds and resilience, often supported by mutual aid societies, trade unions and grassroots movements advocating for better rights and conditions. Literature, journalism and reform campaigns gradually brought attention to their plight, laying the groundwork for future social reforms.

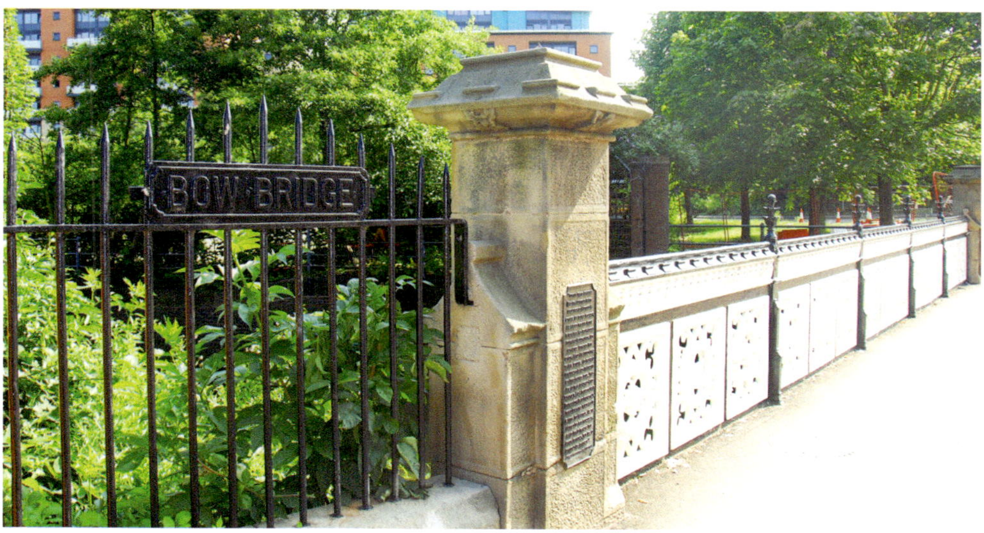

Bow Bridge. A historically significant river crossing and gateway into the town since before the Roman period.

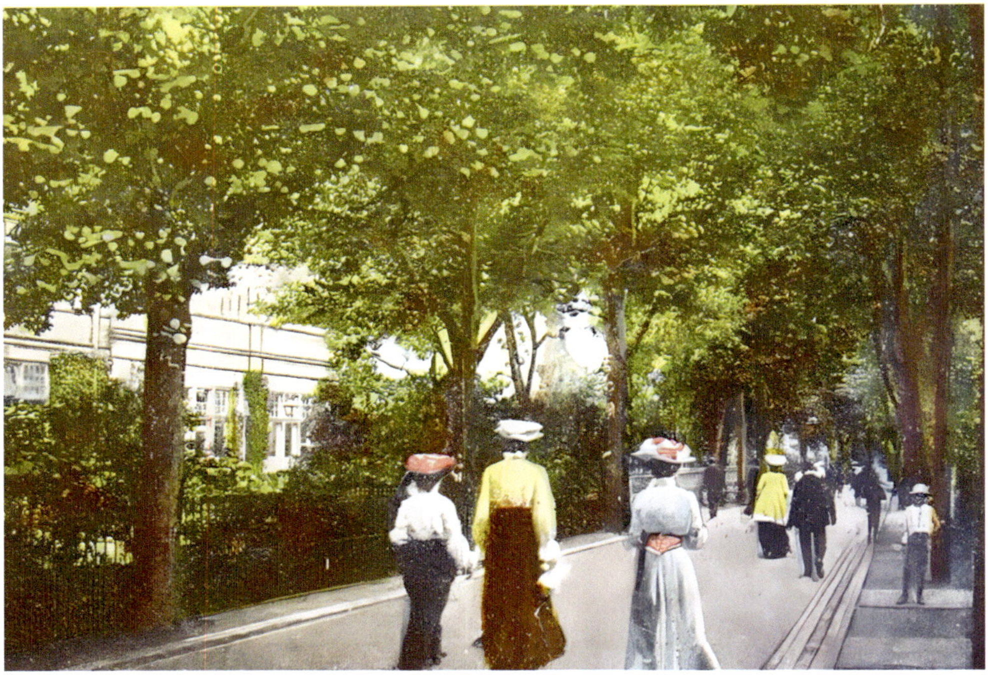

A pleasant perambulation along New Walk, laid out in 1785. It follows the line of the Roman trackway the Via Devana.

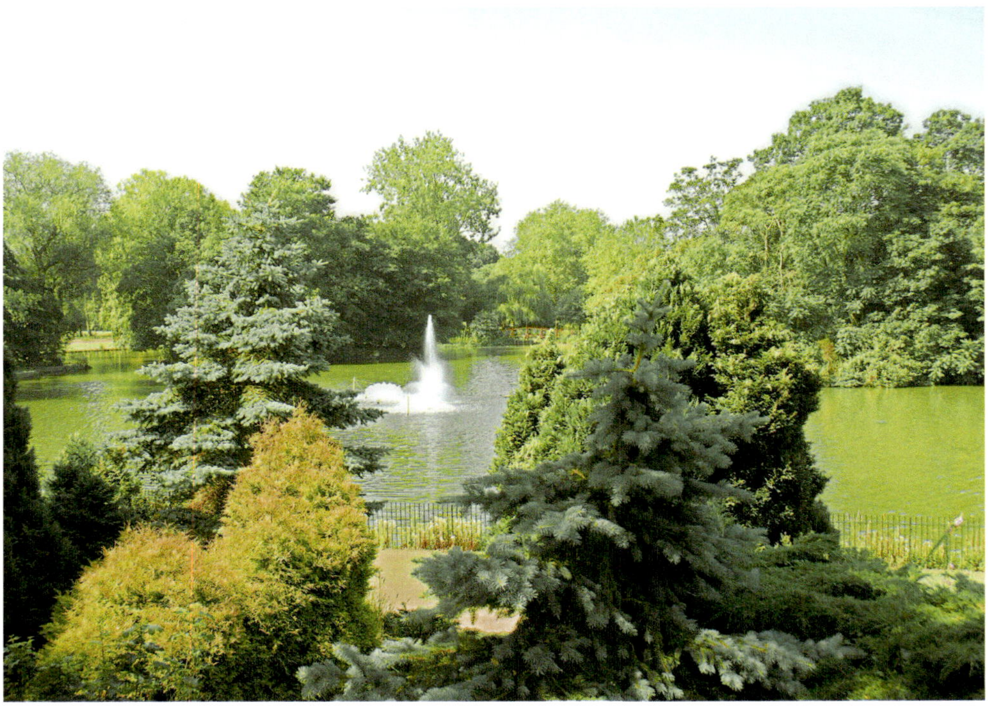

Abbey Park. A tranquil green space near the heart of Leicester with a history dating back to the foundation of Leicester Abbey in 1143.

9

Wartime Leicester

Fourteen years after the war memorial in Victoria Park was completed, honouring those who had given their lives during the First World War, Britain declared war on Germany after the invasion of Poland. The people of Leicester again became part of a global conflict.

Leicester's industrial landscape also shifted dramatically during the war. Traditional industries like hosiery and footwear were disrupted as many male workers joined the military. Factories adapted to wartime needs with companies such as Equity Shoes producing utility footwear. Meanwhile, engineering and electrical industries flourished, manufacturing items for the war effort as diverse as typewriters, electric vehicles, socks, and aero engines. A wartime industrial handbook listed over 150 different products made in Leicester, highlighting the city's vital role in supporting the war effort.

During the war, Corahs at their St Margaret's factory produced 26 million knitted items and processed around 250 million clothing coupons. Their engineering department manufactured 80,000 gun parts and 30,000 parts for tank landing craft. Leicester's machine tools industry provided precision parts for Spitfire engines.

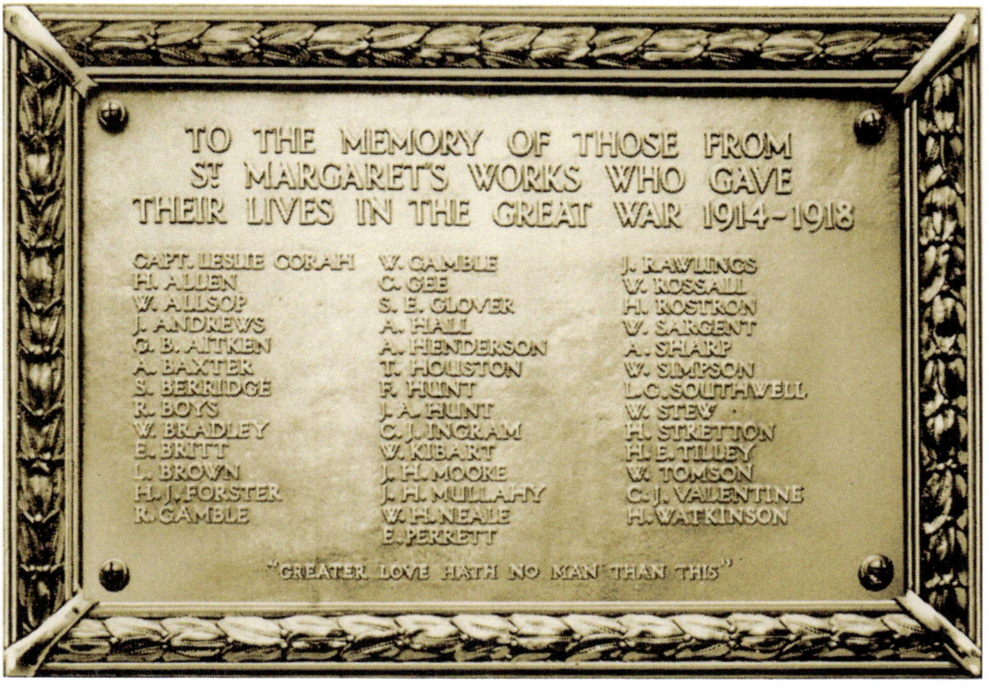

Memorial plaque for employees of Corah's St Margaret's works who lost their lives in the First World War.

British Thomson Houston

In 1939, British Thomson Houston (BTH), based in Rugby, transferred a skeleton staff to Leicester to prepare for the manufacture of munitions. By 1940, fifty staff, mainly women, were employed on the site, building radio location equipment and, later, radar equipment.

Several other companies near to BTH were also involved in wartime manufacture including A. S. Yeates which made parts for Spitfires. Part of the BTH site, where Ravensbridge Drive is now situated, was given over to Nissen huts, and a Home Guard post was built in the vicinity to protect the factory. Older residents of the area remember that until the 1960s, the factory remained, to some extent, under camouflage.

In 1943, the factory played a small but key role in the Dambusters raid on German dams in the Ruhr and Eder valleys. The nineteen Lancaster bombers involved in Operation Chastise were equipped with specially mounted spotlights designed and built in Leicester to enable the pilots and navigators to judge with accuracy their altitude. To be effective, the 'bouncing bombs' designed by Barnes Wallace had to be released when the aircraft were at a precise altitude of 60 feet which was measured by equipment manufactured in Leicester.

Even experienced aircrew found it challenging to maintain level flight at such a low altitude and judge such minimal distances. The popular Dambusters film, released in 1955, suggests that the idea of using spotlights mounted under the aircraft wings at angles

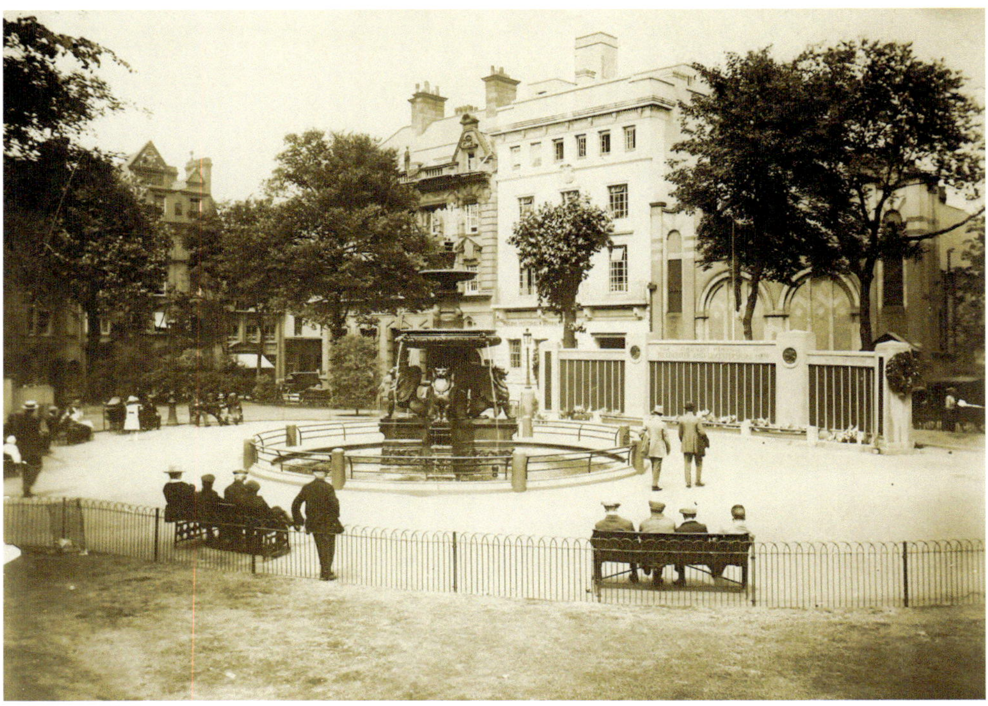

The first memorial to the fallen which was erected in Town Hall Square before the construction of the Arch of Remembrance in Victoria Park.

that meant the beams merged on the ground at exactly 60 feet came from a visit by Guy Gibson to a London theatre where he watched how lighting followed the dancers on stage. In fact, the mechanism was devised by Benjamin Lockspeiser, Deputy Director of Scientific Research at the Ministry of Aircraft production, who remembered that a similar solution had been tried out by RAF Coastal Command earlier in the war to find inshore submarines. This earlier use of converging beams had not been successful because the light was disrupted by waves in tidal waters. However, the surface of the water in the reservoirs was still. Similarly, a special low-level altimeter designed by EMI for the purpose failed to work. The lights required powerful and reliable 40KW generators, and these were manufactured at BTH in Leicester.

BTH continued to supply armaments after the end of the Second World War including guidance systems for Blue Streak anti-aircraft missiles. The factory also made searchlights for Chieftain Tanks between 1963 and 1979 in association with GEC Thorn Lighting in Melton Road.

The Leicester Blitz

Leicester was not spared from the horrors of bombing. The most devastating raid occurred on 19 November 1940 in the Highfields area, where 108 people lost their lives. Bombs struck key buildings such as Saxby Street Methodist Church and St Peter's Church, as well as numerous homes. The city's Air Raid Precautions (ARP) Mobile First Aid Unit, led by Dr Ernest Garrett, responded with bravery and efficiency. Civil defence workers, including firemen and police, played crucial roles during these raids, and several were recognized for their heroism with medals and certificates of merit. Today, modern buildings in Highfields stand where bombed structures once were, marking the legacy of that tragic night.

Mary Attenborough

In 1937 Mary Attenborough, mother of Sir David and Lord Richard Attenborough, led a voluntary committee to establish a hostel at Evington Hall for fifty unaccompanied children from the Basque country in northern Spain. They were refugees from General Franco's Nationalist forces in the Spanish Civil War and among almost 4,000 children who had left the city of Bilbao on the SS *Habana*. The hostel remained open for two years. Mary was passionate in resisting calls for the return of children to situations of danger in Spain until the end of the war. Her commitment was personified in her regular hands-on-her-knees cleaning of the floors at Evington Hall.

The city saw the arrival of evacuees from more heavily bombed areas of England, and residents quickly adapted to wartime conditions. Rationing of food and fuel began early, and 'British Restaurants' were established to provide affordable meals. Women stepped into roles traditionally held by men, working in factories, transport and civil defence, which helped pave the way for future movements toward gender equality.

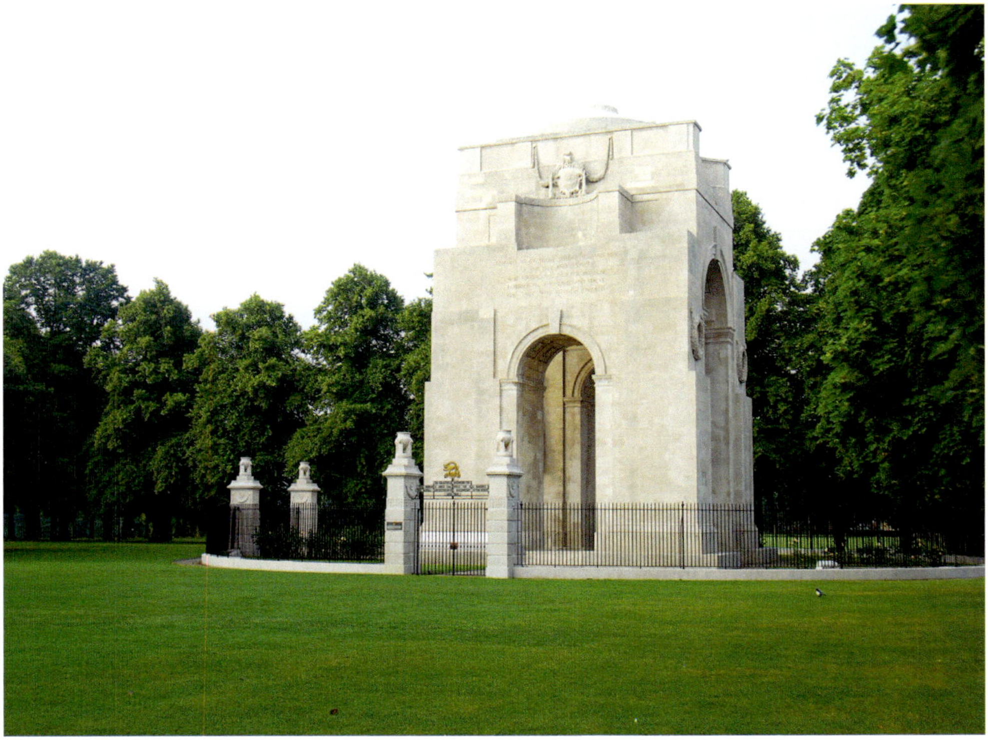

The Arch of Remembrance in Victoria Park, designed by Sir Edwin Lutyens in 1925. It is aligned so that the rising sun shines through its arches on Armistice Day.

The Leicester School of Art

Students at the Leicester School of Art created posters, signage, guidebooks and leaflets for the local Civil Defence Committee and the Publicity and Development Committee. They decorated restaurants, canteens and air raid shelters with murals. The students also prepared models and charts for the Town Reconstruction Committee and provided training courses for members of the Armed Forces.

The Hawthorn Building in the Newarke gave hospitality to distinguished visitors from abroad and Armed Forces personnel. The school also manufactured hospital furniture and equipment for the City Health Department. The Principal, Kenneth Holmes, painted watercolours recording the bomb damage sustained during the Leicester Blitz.

The Leicestershire Regiment

In the Second World War, six battalions of the Leicestershire Regiment served from Norway to Malaya. The regiment received twenty-two battle honours for its outstanding contribution. It became the Royal Leicestershire Regiment in 1946.

The American 82nd Airborne Division, 508th Regiment, was based in Leicester before the D-Day landings in 1944. They flew to Europe from Saltby near Melton Mowbray on 5 June 1944. An engraved rock was placed in Victoria Park to commemorate their service, close to Lutyens' cenotaph.

One Unusual Legacy

During and after the Second World War, meat remained a rationed commodity in Britain, with restrictions continuing until June 1954. In response to the scarcity and the needs of local families, Leicester butcher Henry Walker sought a creative solution to offer his customers an affordable and satisfying alternative. Observing the long queues of housewives outside his shop on Cheapside, Walker began experimenting with frying thick slices of potatoes. This simple yet ingenious idea led to the birth of what would become one of Britain's most iconic snack brands, Walkers Crisps.

Initially intended as a substitute for meat-based products, the crisps quickly gained popularity for their taste and convenience. Walker's innovation not only provided a practical answer to wartime shortages but also laid the foundation for a business that would grow into a household name across the UK.

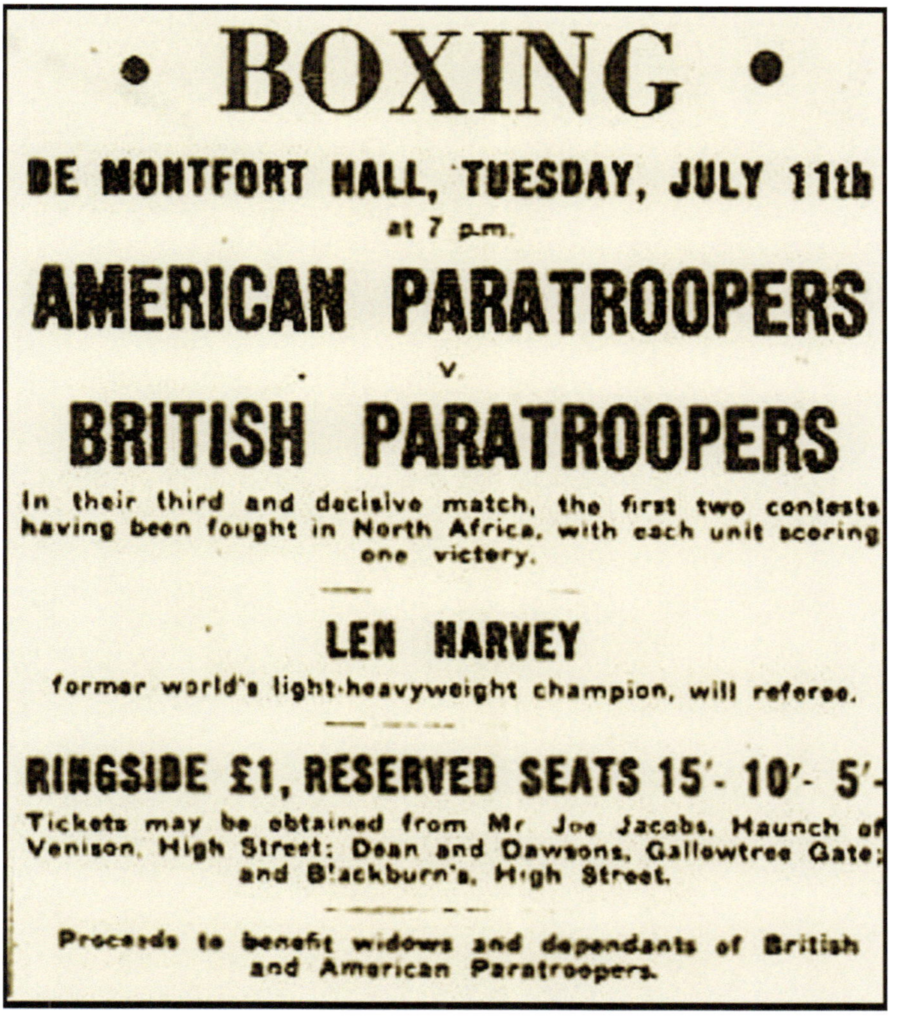

A wartime 'friendly' boxing tournament between British and American boxers at the De Montfort Hall.

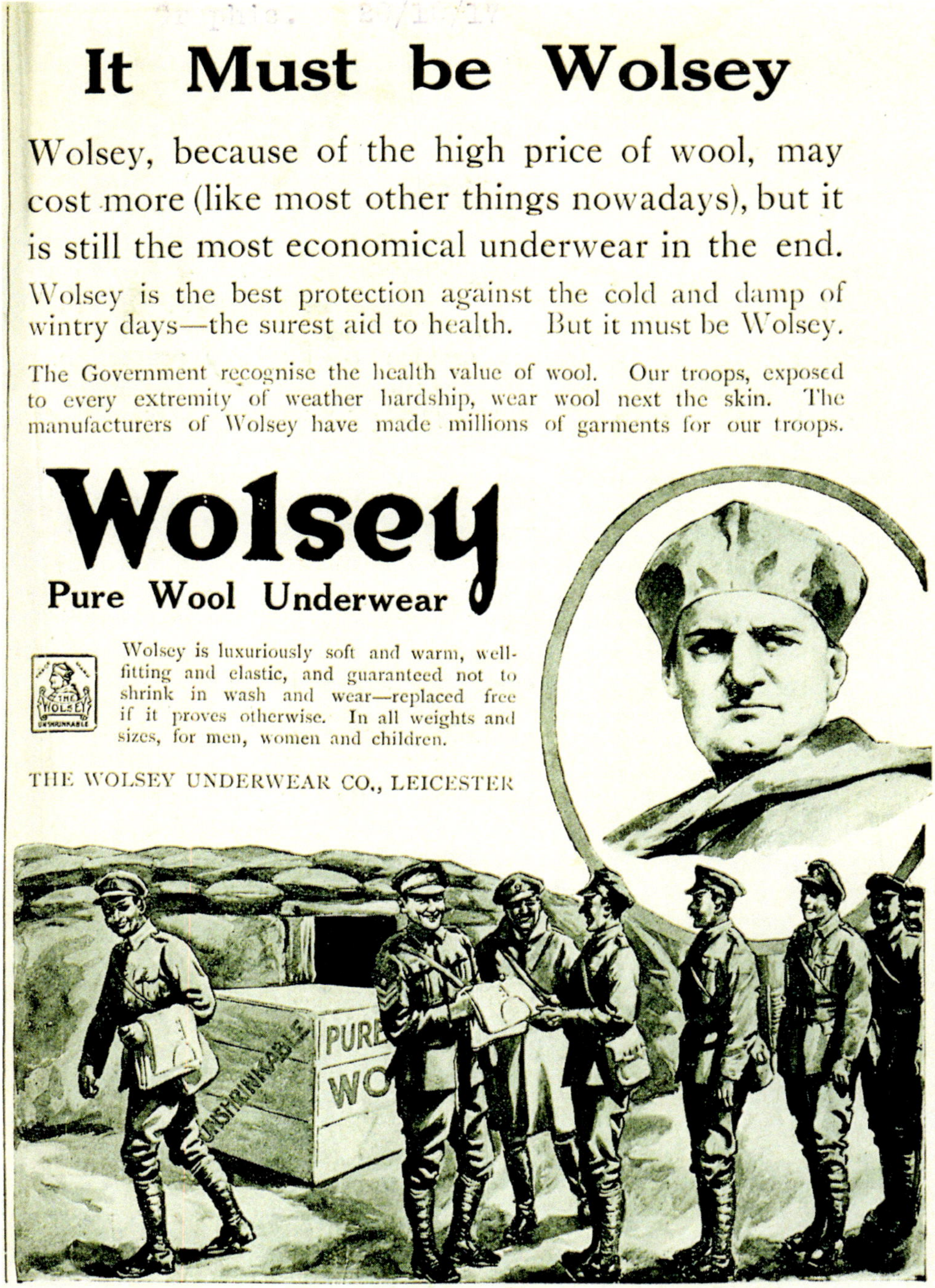

Leicester's oldest textile brand, Wolsey Underwear Ltd, clothing the troops during the First World War.

10

Future, Present and Past

As the world began to take stock of the real cost – in human as well as economic terms – of the Second World War, the 1950s became a decade of change and growth, social, economic and cultural.

The immediate post-war years in Leicester were marked by a pressing need for housing, with an estimated 10,000 homes required to accommodate returning servicemen and displaced families. The city responded by constructing thousands of new homes, including prefabricated houses and large estates including New Parks, Eyres Monsell and Thurnby Lodge. Slum clearance, halted by the conflict, resumed, clearing inner-city areas to make way for modern housing developments.

Economically, a shift began from Leicester's traditional industries of hosiery and footwear towards engineering and electrical manufacturing. The hosiery industry remained strong, and Leicester was still known for 'clothing the world', but the footwear sector began to decline. Engineering saw growth with firms producing a wide range of goods including typewriters, electric vehicles, and aero engines. The city's industrial diversity helped it weather economic fluctuations, and the 1950s are remembered as a time of prosperity and expansion. This diversity continued to protect Leicester in the following decades from the general decline in prosperity experienced by many other cities.

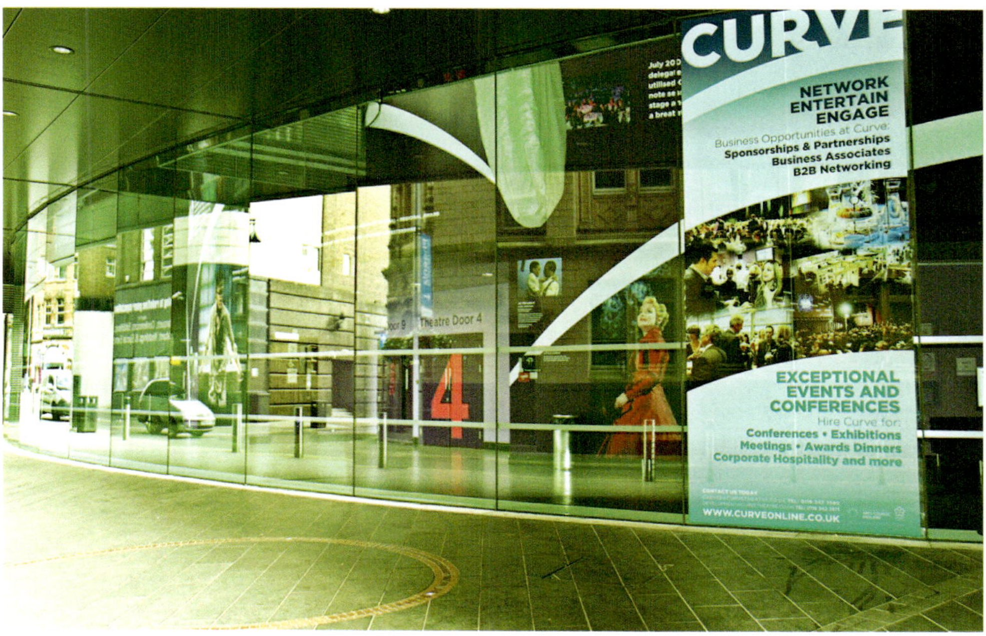

Curve – the window reflecting the world outside as well as the dramas within the theatre.

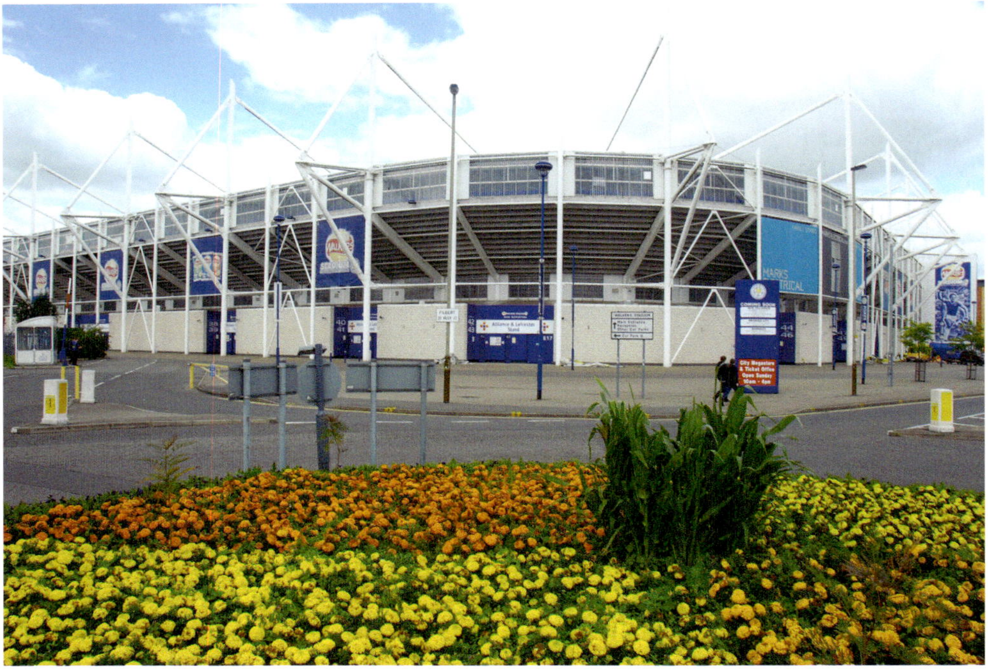

The King Power Stadium opened on 23 July 2002, initially named the Walkers Stadium. It replaced the Filbert Street ground which had served Leicester City fans for more than a century.

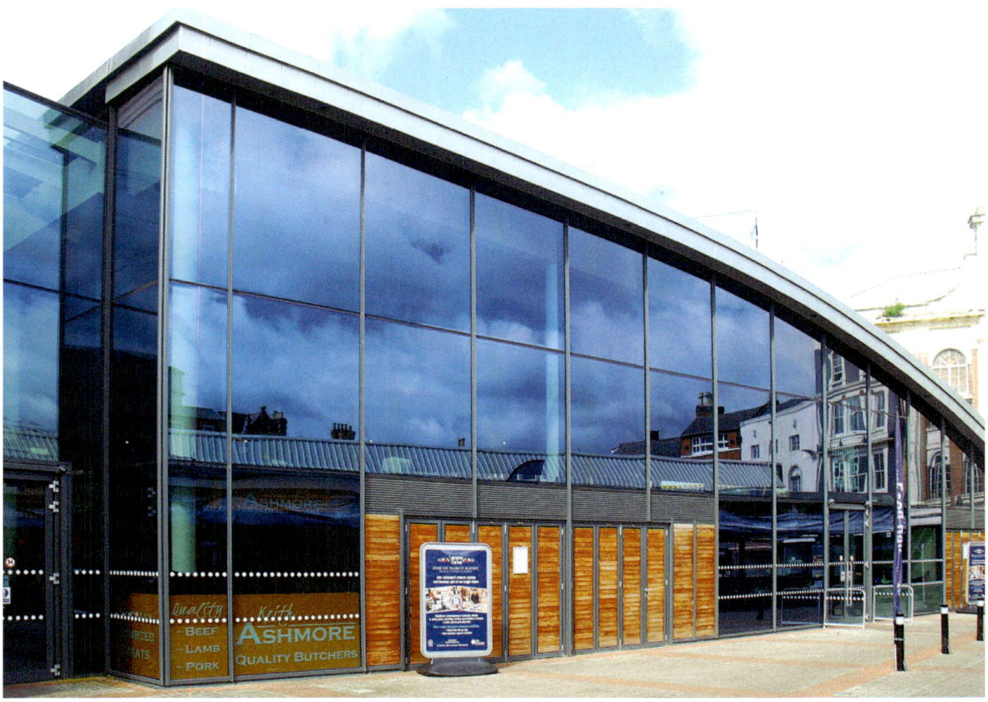

The 'new' indoor market opened in 2014, replacing the former building that had been in place since 1974.

Having a Good Time

In 1957, the Prime Minister, Harold Macmillan, made a speech in Bedford to his fellow Conservatives in which he said, 'Let us be frank about it: most of our people have never had it so good.' In the speech he celebrated the success of Britain's post-war economy while at the same time urging wage restraint and warning against inflation. He was reflecting the stance of the Democratic Party in the United States which had used the same phrase as a slogan in the 1952 US election campaign.

For many, Macmillan's statement rang true. Rationing had finally ended in 1953. British manufacturing was beginning to move from its wartime footing towards new products, and the fledgling National Health Service brought a sense of security to family life.

Released from wartime stringencies, social life in Leicester during the 1950s became vibrant and community oriented. Local shops, cafes and family-run businesses were predominant, even in the centre of the city, and leisure activities including cinema, dance halls and sporting events flourished. However, theatres began to close as television gained popularity, although working men's clubs and societies prospered, offering opportunities for music, sport and adult education. The city also saw the beginnings of comprehensive education and improvements in healthcare, with new clinics and services introduced under the National Health Service.

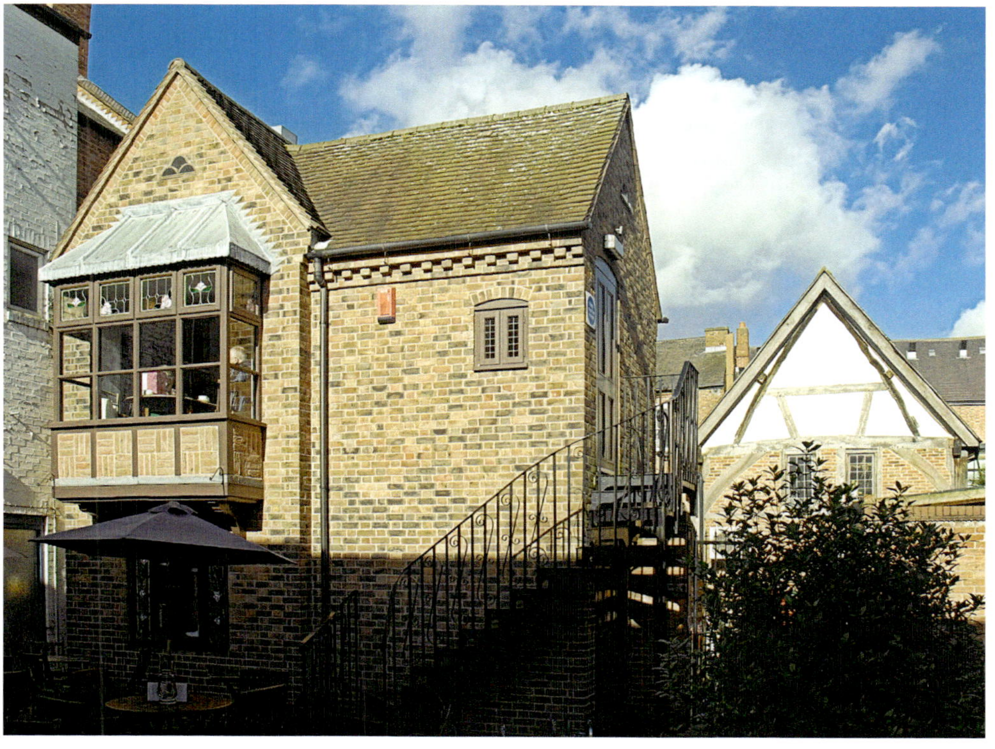

Part of the 'Leicester Lanes' area, the St Martin's shopping precinct opened in 1984. The architectural design intended to harmonise with the older buildings nearby.

The 'Pop' Revolution

The revolution in popular music at the beginning of the 1960s also signalled cultural and social change. The rise of the pirate radio stations such as Radio Caroline, Radio City and Radio London emphasised a widening generation gap between parents listening to the BBC Light Programme and their children who, with increasingly inexpensive and portable transistor radios, were tuning into a range of informal 'DJs' on the pirate stations later to become household names. It took the BBC until 1967 to respond, with the creation of BBC Radio 1.

The Monterey Pop Festival in California in 1967 is regarded as the first major rock festival of this era, and featured Jimmy Hendrix, Janis Joplin and The Who. Two years later, the Isle of Wight festival was the first of many now legendary music events in the UK.

Clubs and music venues in Leicester were busy. Leicester's music and club scene in the 1960s and 1970s was a vibrant reflection of the city's youth culture and musical evolution. Venues including the Il Rondo Ballroom on Silver Street became central to the live music experience, hosting legendary acts such as The Rolling Stones, The Who, Cream and American blues icons like John Lee Hooker and Howlin' Wolf. Other popular spots included The Palais, The Nite Owl and The White Cat Café, which offered dancing and live performances. Coffee bars like The Chameleon, El Casa and El Paso were also key social hubs, staying open late and attracting young people seeking music and community.

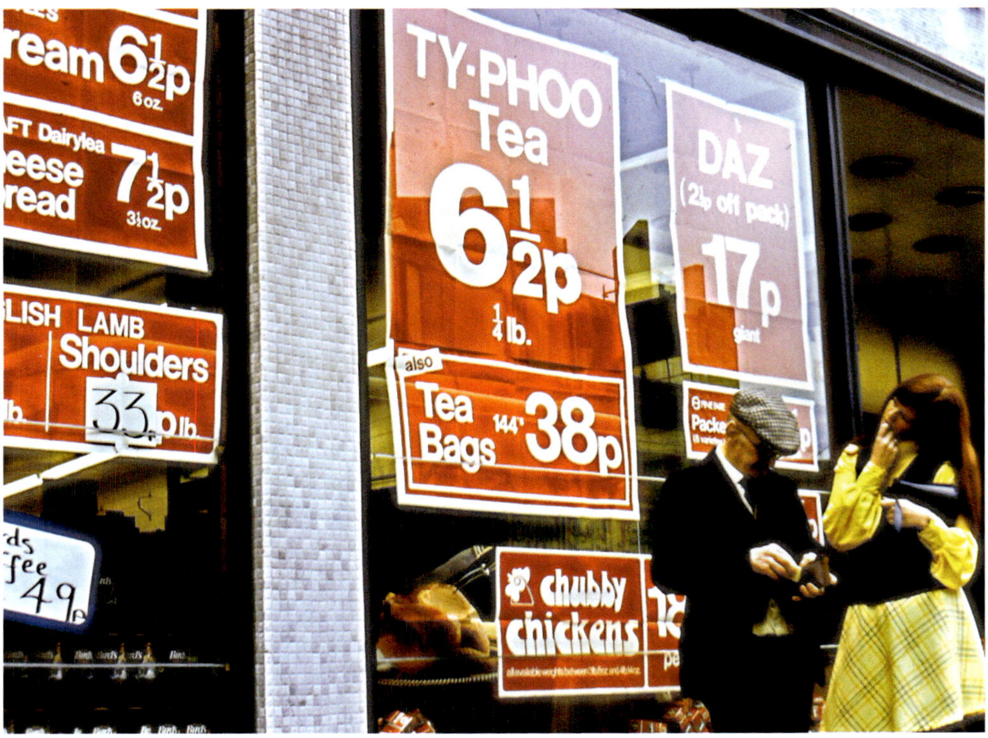

Checking the small change outside the Safeway supermarket in Charles Street on 15 February 1971, Decimalisation Day.

Local bands played a significant role in shaping Leicester's musical identity. Bands like Legacy impressed even Jimi Hendrix, while Family, formed from The Farinas, gained national recognition. Ric Grech, Family's bassist, went on to join Blind Faith with Eric Clapton. Pesky Gee! evolved into Black Widow, known for their theatrical rock style, and The Dallas Boys became one of Leicester's first nationally known pop groups, often seen as early pioneers of the boy band concept. Leicester also contributed to the folk revival, with clubs like the one at the Red Cow pub on Belgrave Gate starting in 1961.

The 1970s saw Leicester's music scene continue to expand and evolve. Engelbert Humperdinck, otherwise known as Gerry Dorsey, became an international star after years of performing in local pubs. Laurel Aitken, the 'Godfather of Ska', settled in Leicester in 1970 and played a key role in the ska revival later in the decade. Showaddywaddy, formed from the merger of two groups in 1973, brought retro rock 'n' roll to the charts and became one of the city's most successful bands.

Nightlife in the 1970s continued to thrive, with clubs like The Burlesque and The Nite Owl offering all-night dancing and becoming central to Leicester's social life. The Hungry I Pancake House, now the Good Earth restaurant, was a jazz hotspot launched by the Monk brothers. Underground and DIY music scenes also began to emerge, laying the groundwork for punk and new wave movements in the following decade.

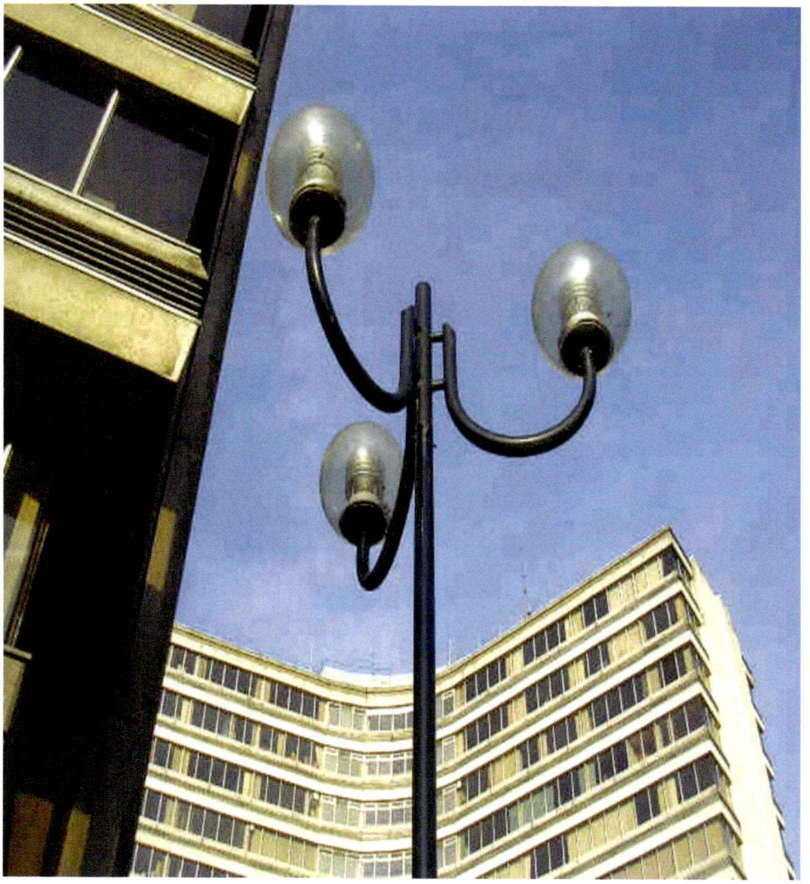

The New Walk Centre was a speculative venture built in 1975, acquired by Leicester City Council. Having been declared structurally unsafe, it was demolished in 2010.

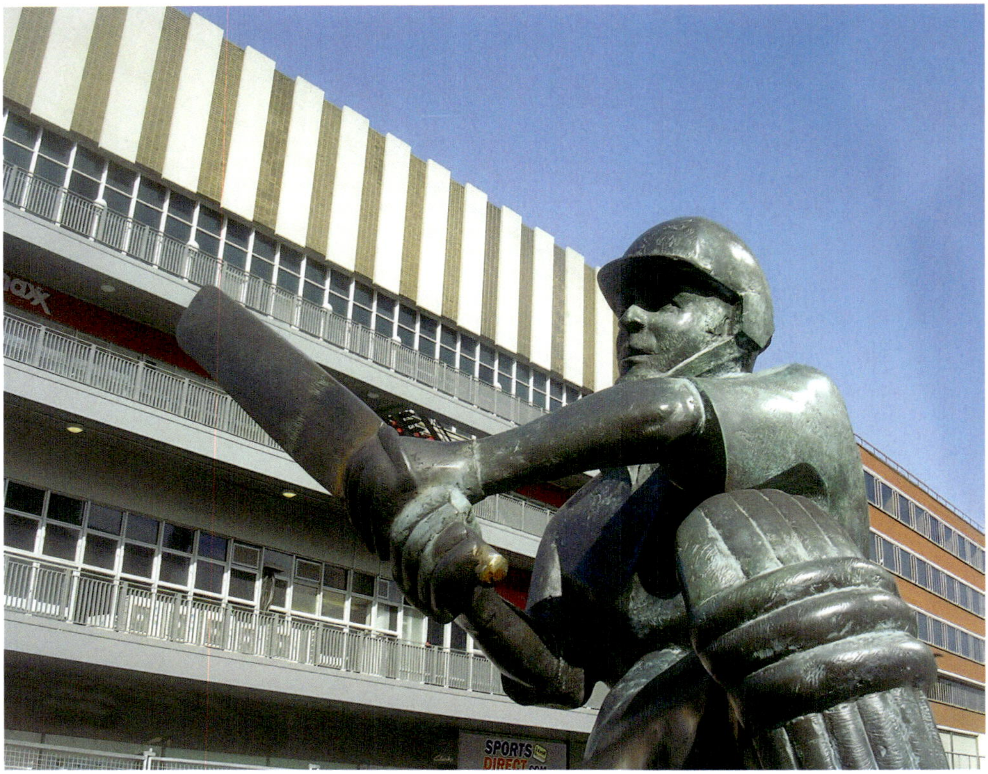

The sports statue in the city centre celebrates three major sports teams: Leicester City Football, Leicester Tigers and Leicestershire County Cricket.

But it was much more than a music revolution. The miniskirt and Alec Issigonis' mini car (both in bright colours!) epitomised a desire by the younger generation to move on, and move forward, and to enjoy life. For many young people in Leicester, London's Carnaby Street was the place to emulate, and in the words of the Beatles, 'all you needed was love'.

Multi-cultural Leicester

Leicester's multi-cultural identity began soon after the war. Though the numbers were modest compared to later decades, the arrival of people from Eastern Europe, Ireland, the Caribbean and South Asia laid the foundation for Leicester's future identity as one of Britain's most multicultural cities. Many newcomers settled in areas like Highfields which had suffered wartime damage where there was consequently available affordable housing. These communities later established cultural and social institutions including Polish schools, Caribbean sports clubs and religious centres.

Asian immigration to Leicester during the 1960s and 1970s significantly transformed the city's demographic, cultural and economic landscape. The migration occurred in two major waves, from the Indian subcontinent in the 1960s, and later from East Africa, particularly Uganda, in the early 1970s.

Many of these early arrivals were economic migrants drawn by the promise of employment in the city's thriving textile and manufacturing industries. They often took up low-paid, labour-intensive jobs.

The most dramatic shift came in 1972, when Ugandan dictator Idi Amin ordered the expulsion of the country's Asian population, giving them just ninety days to leave. Many were British passport holders, descendants of Indians who had migrated to East Africa during British colonial rule. Despite a publicity campaign by Leicester City Council discouraging them from settling in the city, fearing a strain on public services, thousands of Ugandan Asians chose Leicester as their new home.

By the end of the 1970s, Leicester had received over 20,000 East African Asians, more than any other British city. These were often highly skilled and entrepreneurial peoples. Many had run successful businesses in Uganda and were therefore quick to re-establish themselves in Leicester, opening shops, restaurants and service-based enterprises. Their arrival revitalised areas like Belgrave and Melton Road, which became known for their vibrant South Asian culture, earning the nickname 'The Golden Mile'.

Despite their contributions, the new immigrants faced significant challenges. Many encountered racism, discrimination in housing and employment, and cultural isolation. Oral histories from the East Midlands Oral History Archive reveal stories of hardship, resilience and gradual integration. Over time, the community was able to build strong support networks, and institutions like the BBC Asian Network helped to give voice to their culture.

By the late 1970s, Leicester had become a model of multiculturalism, with a thriving South Asian population playing a central role in the city's economy and cultural life. The legacy of this migration is visible today in Leicester's diverse communities, festivals and businesses.

Our 'Golden Age'

What happened yesterday is history, and today will become history by tomorrow. Time, and our perception of it, has long fascinated writers from H. G. Wells to Arthur C. Clarke who imagined worlds where people could travel forward or backward through time. When we look at photographs of Leicester from previous decades and centuries, it is common to desire a return to a 'golden age', a time when the city seemed perfect: no litter, no vandalism, everyone smartly dressed, it was safe to walk the streets after dark and the shopping centre was bustling with life.

Each of us remembers a 'golden age', often tied to the years when we first became aware of the world around us. For some, it might be the 1950s; for others, the 1960s or later. This idealised perception of Leicester is shaped by personal experience, seen through the eyes of one individual at a particular moment in time. It is your history – and mine.

If understanding the past helps us make sense of the present, then historians carry the responsibility of presenting an objective account. Yet true objectivity is elusive. We may recall the comforting presence of a local doctor making house calls, but not remember the fear of diseases like diphtheria, smallpox and polio. Do we remember the iron lungs used at Groby Road Hospital? We might cherish memories of camaraderie in the factories, but

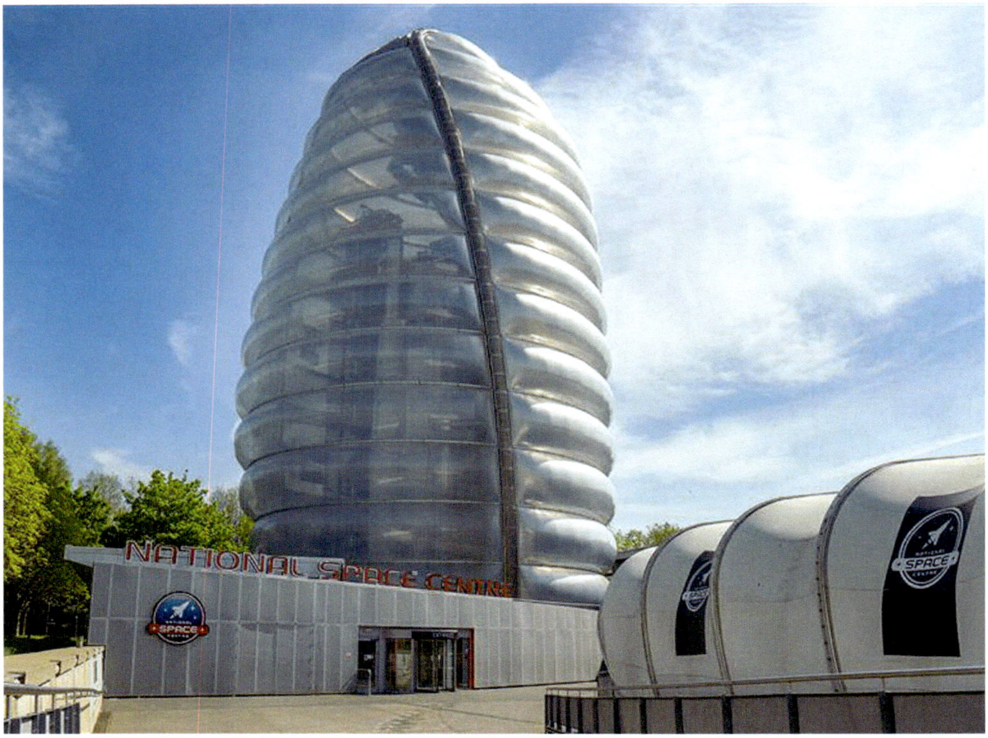

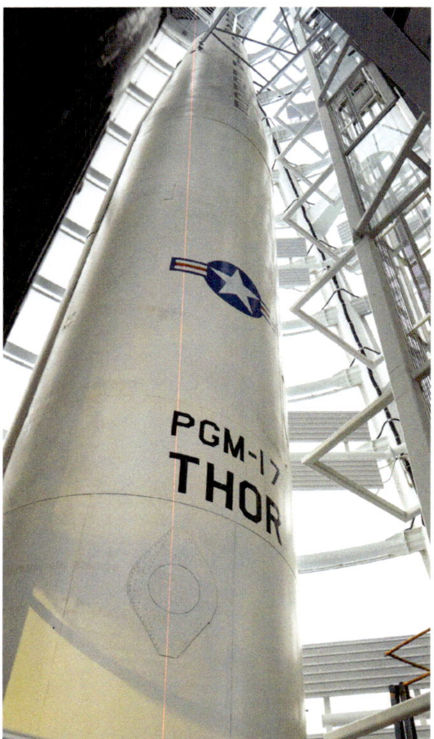

Above, left and overleaf: The Space Centre, not only a local attraction but a national amenity, tells the story of space travel in a dramatic hands-on style. (Courtesy of the National Space Centre)

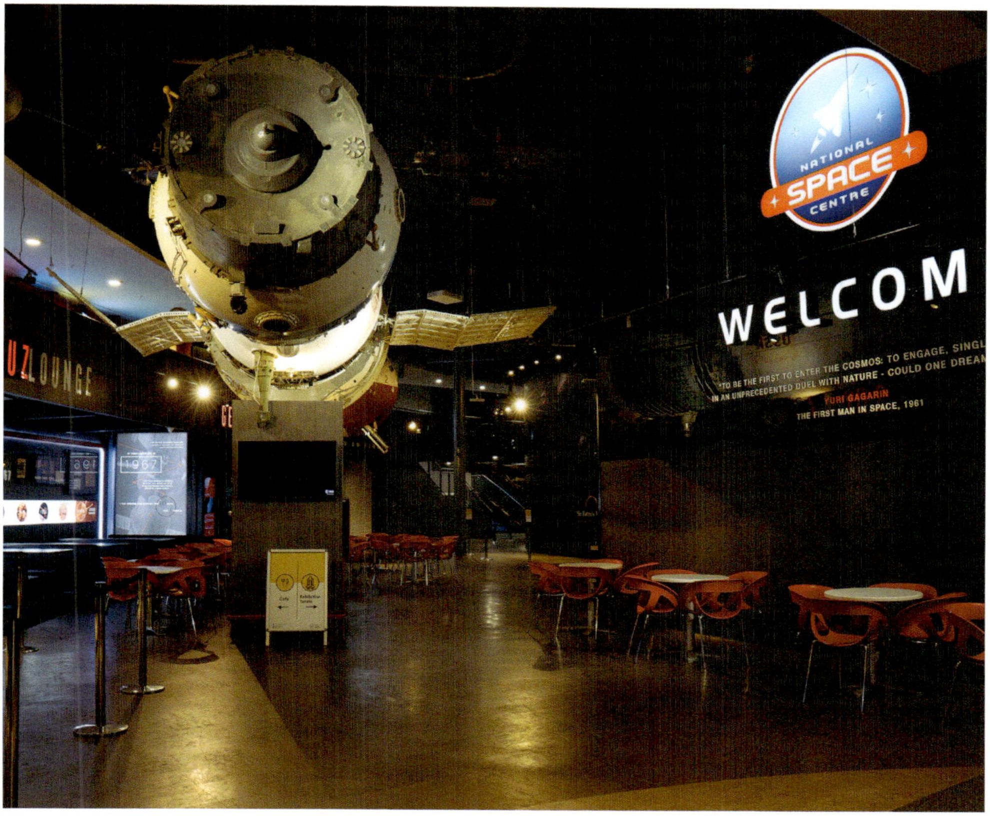
NATIONAL
SPACE
CENTRE
WELCOM
"TO BE THE FIRST TO ENTER THE COSMOS: TO ENGAGE, SINGL
IN AN UNPRECEDENTED DUEL WITH NATURE - COULD ONE DREAM
YURI GAGARIN
THE FIRST MAN IN SPACE, 1961
UZLOUNGE

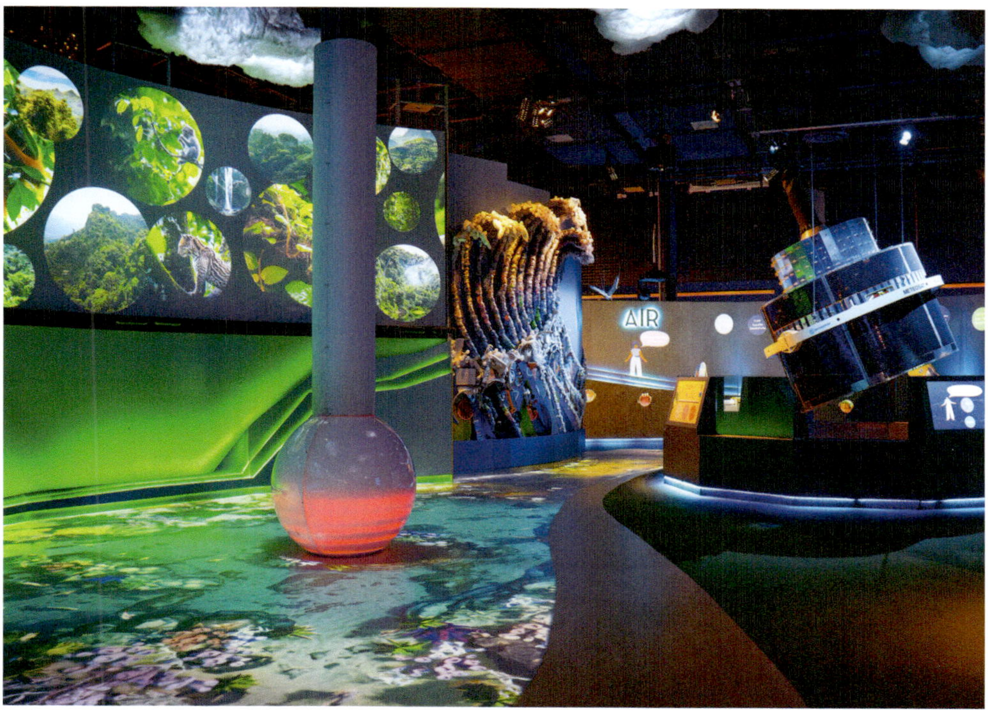
AIR

do we remember the many workers who were injured or killed in industrial accidents? And what of our schoolmates who, due to physical or mental disabilities, were cruelly labelled, sometimes beaten, and excluded?

We must be cautious not to judge the past by today's standards. The world, and Leicester, has changed dramatically in the first quarter-century since the Millennium. The most transformative force has been the rise of internet technology which has reshaped how we live, communicate and perceive the world. Whether through social media or the ever-present smartphone, our lives are continuously influenced by digital innovation.

If someone were to write a concise history of Leicester in the twenty-second century, how might they interpret the events of today?

Recent history has seen Leicester face challenges familiar to many cities across England. It was the first to undergo a Covid-related lockdown, and its retail heart has felt the strain of online shopping and economic pressures. Yet, amid these difficulties, new industries have quietly emerged, harnessing cutting-edge technologies.

Leicester remains a vital hub for retail distribution, thanks to its strategic location near major motorways and airports. And yes, it proudly retains its title as the potato crisp and pie capital of the country!

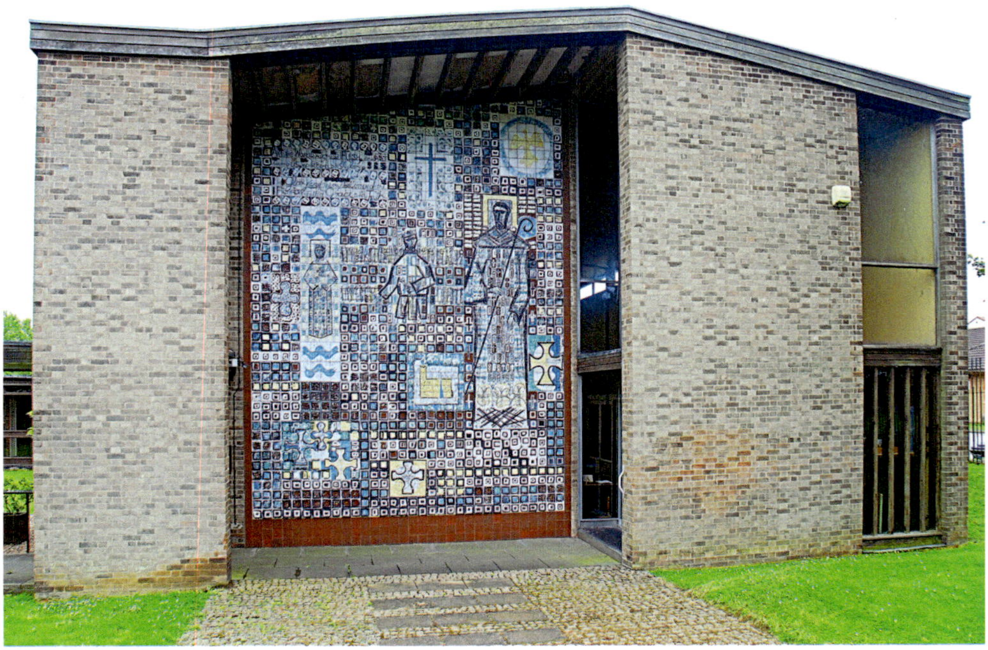

St Aidan's Parish Church, built in 1959 on the New Parks Estate. The architect was Sir Basil Spence.

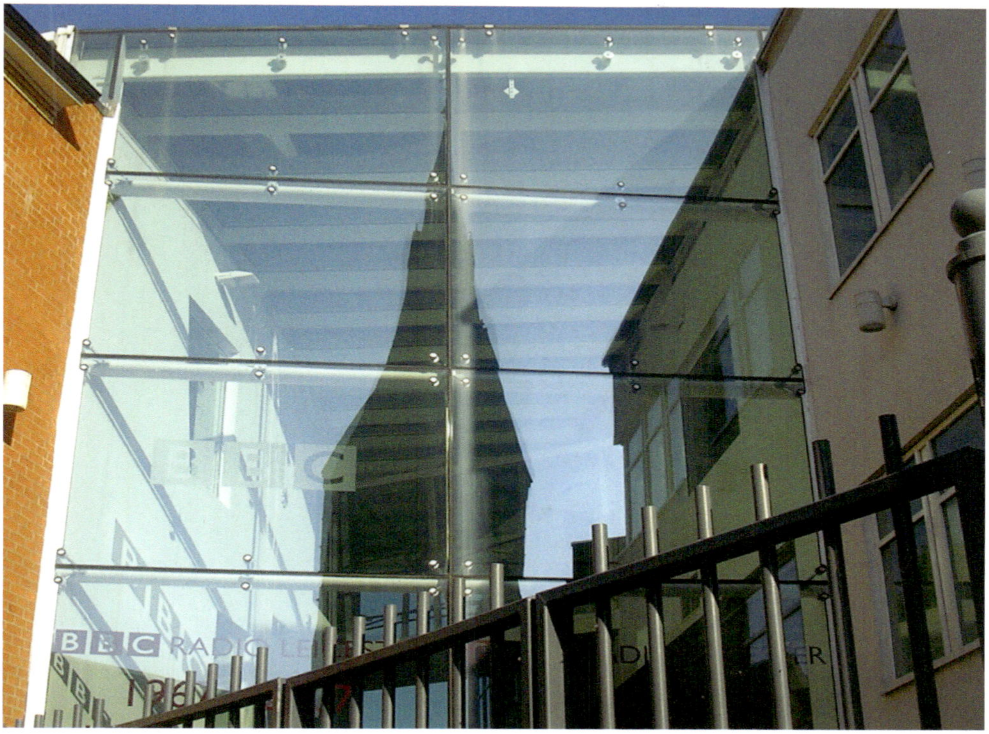

The spire of St Martin's Cathedral seen from the atrium of the BBC studios in St Nicholas Place.

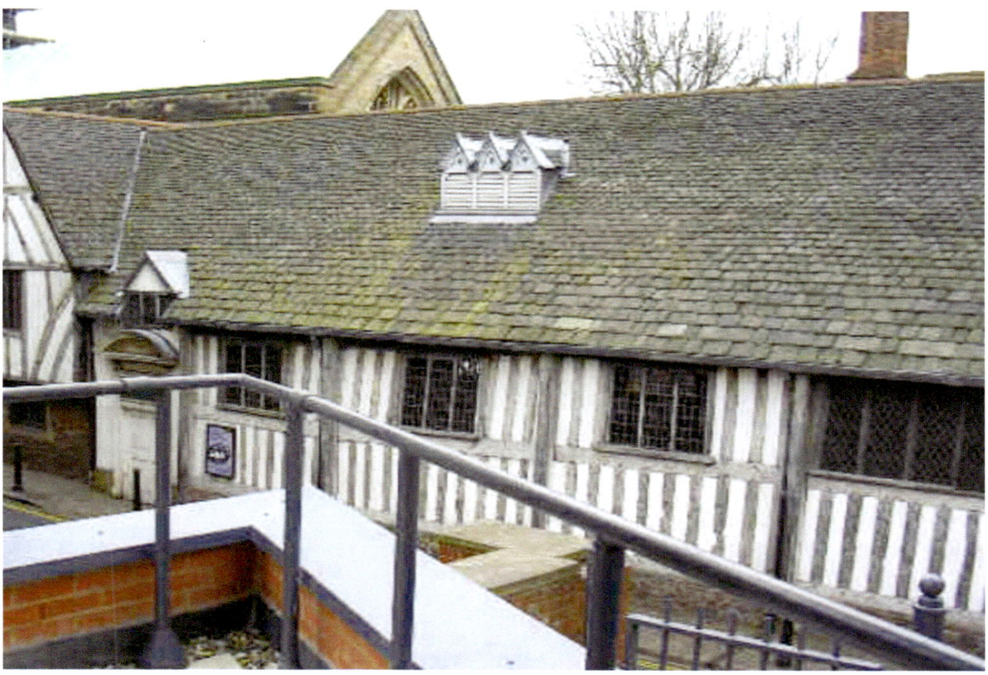

Angles old and new: the cathedral and the Guildhall viewed from the first-floor balcony of the BBC studios.

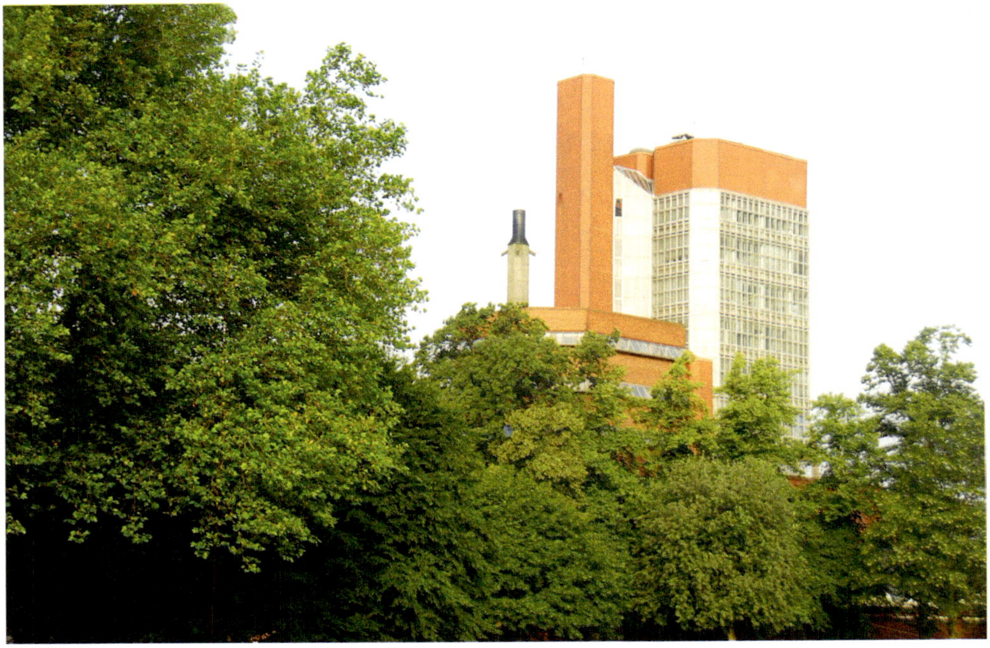

The Stirling and Gowan building on the Leicester University campus. Completed in 1963, the tower is an iconic landmark viewed across Victoria Park.